Nonfiction
for
Middle School

Nonfiction
for
Middle School

A Sentence-Composing Approach

A Student Worktext

Don and Jenny Killgallon

HEINEMANN
Portsmouth, NH

Heinemann
361 Hanover Street
Portsmouth, NH 03801–3912
www.heinemann.com

Offices and agents throughout the world

Library of Congress Cataloging-in-Publication Data
Names: Killgallon, Don, author. | Killgallon, Jenny, author.
Title: Nonfiction for middle school : a sentence-composing approach : a
   student worktext / Don and Jenny Killgallon.
Description: Portsmouth, NH : Heinemann, 2016.
Identifiers: LCCN 2015041414 | ISBN 9780325062891
Subjects: LCSH: English language—Composition and exercises—Study and
   teaching (Middle school). | English language—Sentences—Study and teaching
   (Middle school).
Classification: LCC LB1631 .K4695 2016 | DDC 428.0071/2—dc23

LC record available at http://lccn.loc.gov/2015041414

Editor: Tobey Antao
Production: Hilary Goff & Patty Adams
Cover and interior designs: Monica Ann Crigler
Typesetter: Cape Cod Compositors, Inc.
Manufacturing: Steve Bernier

Printed in the United States of America on acid-free paper
20   19   18   17   16   PPC   1   2   3   4   5

CONTENTS

NONFICTION: WORDS, SENTENCES, PARAGRAPHS

Throughout this worktext, you will learn the meanings of words in context within featured nonfiction selections, read brief excerpts of nonfiction, and learn how their authors build sentences and paragraphs. You will participate in an apprenticeship in the reading and writing of nonfiction.

SENTENCE TOOLS FOR NONFICTION

Putting things in the right places requires skill—in your room, your locker, or your sentences. When you learn where nonfiction authors place their sentence-composing tools, you'll also skillfully put those tools in the right places in your own sentences.

SENTENCE BOUNDARIES

Sentences need clear boundaries to tell your readers where one sentence ends and the next sentence begins. In this section, you'll study how inexperienced writers sometimes go "out of bounds" by writing too much sentence or too little. You'll learn to detect, eliminate, and avoid three sentence boundary problems: the fragment, the comma splice, and the run-on.

A SAMPLER OF REMARKABLE NONFICTION

In these sections, featuring brief excerpts from remarkable nonfiction, you'll put your new sentence-composing tools to work to build strong sentences and paragraphs.

Nothing is more satisfying than to write a good sentence.

—Barbara Tuchman, two-time winner of the Pulitzer prize for nonfiction

Nonfiction writing is made up of paragraphs. Paragraphs are made up of sentences. Sentences are made up of words. Sentences and the words they contain—the building blocks of meaning in nonfiction—are sometimes challenging to understand, often because of unfamiliar words.

Take this sentence by Rudolph Giuliani, then mayor of New York City, addressing the General Assembly of the United Nations on October 1, 2001, condemning the tragedy of terrorist attacks on September 11, 2001.

> *There's no moral way to sympathize*
> *with grossly immoral actions.*

Perhaps a problem is the word *moral* and its opposite *immoral*. The meaning of the sentence is roughly this: *There's no [SOMETHING] way to sympathize with grossly [SOMETHING] actions.* What way? What actions? There's no way to tell just from context—other than that something is pretty gross. Maybe it's time-out for dictionary diving to find out what *moral* means (and its opposite *immoral*).

When you take the plunge, here's what you'll find, the full definition from the Merriam-Webster Dictionary:

¹mor·al *adjective* \\'mor-əl, 'mär-\\

: concerning or relating to what is right and wrong in human behavior
: based on what you think is right and good
: considered right and good by most people: agreeing with a standard of right behavior

Full Definition of MORAL
1
a : of or relating to principles of right and wrong in behavior: ETHICAL <*moral* judgments>
b : expressing or teaching a conception of right behavior <a *moral* poem>
c : conforming to a standard of right behavior
d : sanctioned by or operative on one's conscience or ethical judgment <a *moral* obligation>
e : capable of right and wrong action <a *moral* agent>

2
: probable though not proved : VIRTUAL <a *moral* certainty>
3
: perceptual or psychological rather than tangible or practical in nature or effect <a *moral* victory> <*moral* support>
— **mor·al·ly** *adverb*

Examples of MORAL
1. The author avoids making *moral* judgments.
2. Each story teaches an important *moral* lesson.
3. He felt that he had a *moral* obligation to help the poor.
4. We're confident she has the *moral* fiber to make the right decision.
5. Their behavior was not *moral*.
6. Animals are not *moral* creatures and are not responsible for their actions.
7. Nor did these lawyers and bankers walk about suffused with guilt. They had the *moral* equivalent of Teflon on their soul. Church on Sunday, foreclose on Monday.
   —Norman Mailer, *New York Review of Books*, 27 March 2002

Origin of MORAL
Middle English, from Anglo-French, from Latin *moralis*, from *mor-*, *mos* custom
First Known Use: 14th century

Related to MORAL
Synonyms
all right, decent, ethical, honest, honorable, just, good, nice, right, righteous, right-minded, straight, true, upright, virtuous
Antonyms
bad, black, dishonest, dishonorable, evil, evil-minded, immoral, indecent, sinful, unethical, unrighteous, wicked, wrong

Synonym Discussion of MORAL
MORAL, ETHICAL, VIRTUOUS, RIGHTEOUS, NOBLE mean conforming to a standard of what is right and good. MORAL implies conformity to established sanctioned codes or accepted notions of right and wrong <the basic *moral* values of a community>. ETHICAL may suggest the involvement of more difficult or subtle questions of rightness, fairness, or equity <committed to the highest *ethical* principles>. VIRTUOUS implies moral excellence in character <not a religious person, but *virtuous* nevertheless>. RIGHTEOUS stresses guiltlessness or blamelessness and often suggests the sanctimonious <wished to be *righteous* before God and the world>. NOBLE implies moral eminence and freedom from anything petty, mean, or dubious in conduct and character <had the *noblest* of reasons for seeking office>.

Other Philosophy Terms
dialectic, dualism, epistemology, existentialism, metaphysics, ontology, sequitur, solipsism, transcendentalism

Rhymes with MORAL
aural, chloral, choral, coral, floral, laurel, oral, quarrel, sorrel

SOURCE: www.merriam-webster.com/dictionary/moral

Whew! You took the plunge—a deep, long dive, probably finding more than you really wanted to know about the word *moral*, including—in the unlikely event that you were wondering—its origin from the Latin word *moralis*.

Throughout this worktext when individual words are **bold** [*darkened*], a fast definition—a quickshot—will be **adjacent** [*beside it*] in brackets. If you already know the word, just skip ahead. If you don't know the word or aren't sure, the quickshot, though not a full definition of the word, will get you through the sentence without stumbling.

Though not the best seat in the theatre, a quickshot will at least allow you to see the stage. As a result, you can avoid a deep dictionary plunge and keep reading, stumble-free. Try it.

----

*There's no **moral** [right] way to sympathize*
*with grossly **immoral** [wrong] actions.*

Quickshots are a fast glance at a passable but not perfect meaning. For example, you now know that *moral* means right, *immoral* means wrong. Know also that *moral* and *immoral* apply only to human behavior being right or wrong. If you got most of the words right on a spelling test, you wouldn't say, "I got most spellings moral, but some immoral." Spellings aren't human behavior. People behave, not words, so only people can behave morally (rightly) or immorally (wrongly).

Challenges to your understanding of difficult nonfiction come from various factors, including sentence length and structure, but also from the words themselves. Often, if you don't know the words, you don't understand the sentence.

Take a look at an extreme example in this next sentence. *Ontogeny recapitulates phylogeny.*

This sentence has just three words, but unless you know the meaning of each, you won't understand the sentence. Whoever wrote that sentence is sending you its meaning, but you're not receiving it because of a vocabulary block stopping the meaning from getting through.

---

ontogeny: (noun) the development of an individual from a fertilized ovum to maturity, as contrasted with the development of a group or species

recapitulates: (verb) to repeat stages from the evolution of the species during the embryonic period of an animal's life

phylogeny: (noun) the development over time of a species, genus, or group, as contrasted with the development of an individual

---

Whew! Solving that three-word sentence-puzzle is challenging.

Here's the quickshot version: **Ontogeny** [*individual characteristics*] **recapitulates** [*reflect*] **phylogeny** [*species characteristics*]. In other words, an individual reflects the characteristics of the group to which the individual belongs: a duck has the characteristics of duckdom; a cow, cowdom; a chicken, chickendom! If it looks, walks, and quacks like a duck, it must be a duck—and not a giraffe!

Puzzle solved.

Give quickshots a try. Read the following excerpts about paper grocery bags, paying special attention to the meanings of the bolded words and their quickshot definitions. Then complete the activity that follows it.

(1) How do you bag items on a conveyor belt full of ever-changing merchandise? (2) Naturally, harder and heavier things, like cans of vegetables and soup, are properly put in first, providing a solid **base** [*bottom*] that will also give the full bag a low center of gravity. (3) Boxes of macaroni, cake mix, and the like also provide solid **foundations** [*bottoms*] on which to pack smaller, lighter, and **flimsier** [*fragile*] items, like packages of Jell-O and plastic bags of beans. (4) Bread and eggs naturally belong on the very top, but not so far up that they can tumble out when the bag is **grasped** [*held*] and lifted. (5) As obvious as such **protocols** [*procedures*] might be, they were often **violated** [*abused*] by inexperienced, careless, **distracted** [*inattentive*], **malicious** [*mean*], or **mischievous** [*trouble-making*] baggers.

(6) The **overzealous** [*extreme*] bagger who tries to squeeze a box of cat food in beside the other boxes already in the bag can often tear a gash along the side. (7) But for the tough structure, this is usually a **benign** [*harmless*] failure, which only prevents the bag's reuse. (8) It is the grocery bag that is **overly** [*excessively*] heavy because of a **jumble** [*mixture*] of cans and jars and bottles inside that poses the more dangerous situation. (9) There is a **tendency** [*likelihood*] to pick up a bag by its edges, which can usually be done safely only for a light load. (10) The overly heavy bag has a tendency to rip at the **stress-concentration** [*weak*] points beneath one's grasping fingers, a situation that . . . occurs as the bag is being lifted out of the shopping cart beside one's car trunk. (11) The result can be a mess of glass and jelly on the pavement of the parking lot. (12) Like any **design** [*plan*], the so-called perfected grocery bag is only as good as the care with which it is used.

Henry Petroski, *Small Things Considered:*
Why There Is No Perfect Design

ACTIVITY 1: PROVING CLAIMS

Tell whether the claim about paper grocery bags is true or false. Prove your answer by identifying a sentence as evidence for your answer.

1. The best place for canned items is in the middle of the grocery bag.

2. Heavy items placed on the bottom of a full grocery bag provide a low center of gravity.

3. Delicate groceries are best placed in a bag between boxed groceries.

4. Baggers frequently pack bags poorly.

5. Sometimes bags are intentionally packed poorly.

6. Boxes packed too close together can cause a paper grocery bag to tear.

7. Most bad accidents result from squeezing too many boxes together within one grocery bag.

8. Most people carry full grocery bags by lifting them from the bottom.

9. Fewer accidents happen with grocery bags when baggers and carriers are careful.

10. Even with the best grocery bags, accidents happen when people who fill or carry them are careless.

ACTIVITY 2: CHOOSING QUICKSHOTS

First, read the passage below and, *without consulting a dictionary*, choose the best quickshot in the multiple-choice items below according to the context of the passage. Second, *after consulting a dictionary*, confirm or change your choices.

- -

This passage was written by John Adams, one of the framers of the Declaration of Independence and the second President of the United States. Adams explains to Thomas Jefferson, one of the five members on the committee to draft that document,

why Jefferson and not himself should actually write the document that declared the
independence of the thirteen colonies from England.

- -

(1) Mr. Jefferson came into Congress, in June, 1775, and brought with him a **reputation** for literature, science, and a **happy** talent of **composition**. (2) Jefferson's writings were **handed about**, remarkable for the **peculiar felicity** of **expression**. (3) Though a silent member in Congress, Jefferson was so prompt, frank, **explicit**, and **decisive** upon committees and in conversation that he soon **seized** my heart. (4) Upon this occasion I gave Jefferson my vote to head our committee on **independence**, and did all in my power to **procure** the votes of others. (5) I think Jefferson had one more vote than any other, and that placed him at the head of the committee. (6) I had the next highest number, and that placed me second. (7) The committee met, discussed the subject, and then appointed Mr. Jefferson and me to make the **draft** of a **document** on independence, I suppose because we were the two first on the list. (8) The subcommittee met. (9) Jefferson proposed to me to make the draft.

(10) I said, "I will not."

(11) Jefferson said, "You should do it."

(12) I replied, "Oh! No."

(13) "Why will you not? You ought to do it."

(14) "I will not."

(15) "Why?"

(16) "Reasons enough."

(17) "What can be your reasons?"

(18) "Reason first, Mr. Jefferson, you are a Virginian, and a Virginian ought to appear at the head of this **business**. (19) Reason second, I am **obnoxious**, suspected, and unpopular, but you are very

much **otherwise**. (20) Reason third, you can write ten times better than I can."

(21) "Well," said Jefferson, "if you are decided, I will do as well as I can."

(22) "Very well. (23) When you have **drawn** it up, we will have a meeting."

John Adams, "Letter on Thomas Jefferson,"
in *Adams on Adams* (adapted)

Directions: Choose the best quickshot for the context, and then check a dictionary to see if your choice is correct.

- -

Mr. Jefferson came into Congress, in June, 1775, and brought with him a **reputation** for literature, science, and a **happy** talent of **composition**.

- -

1. *Reputation* most nearly means
   a. character

   b. stature

   c. knowledge

   d. meaning.

2. *Happy* most nearly means
   a. probable

   b. mediocre

   c. difficult

   d. useful.

3. *Composition* most nearly means

    a. writing

    b. structuring

    c. denying

    d. criticizing.

Jefferson's writings were **handed about**, remarkable for the **peculiar felicity** of **expression**.

---

4. *Handed about* most nearly means

    a. denied

    b. shared

    c. explained

    d. contradicted.

5. *Peculiar* most nearly means

    a. unique

    b. usual

    c. predictable

    d. strange.

6. *Felicity* most nearly means

    a. eloquence

    b. style

   c. appropriateness

   d. relevance.

7. *Expression* most nearly means
   a. organizing

   b. thinking

   c. revising

   d. communicating.

Though a silent member in Congress, Jefferson was so prompt, frank, **explicit**, and **decisive** upon committees and in conversation that he soon **seized** my heart.

---

8. *Explicit* most nearly means
   a. troublesome

   b. clear

   c. legal

   d. frank.

9. *Decisive* most nearly means
   a. stubborn

   b. obstinate

   c. certain

   d. strong.

10. *Seized* most nearly means

    a. took

    b. possessed

    c. won

    d. tamed.

Upon this occasion I gave Jefferson my vote to head our committee on **independence**, and did all in my power to **procure** the votes of others.

---

11. *Independence* most nearly means

    a. declaration

    b. government

    c. strength

    d. separation.

12. *Procure* most nearly means

    a. acquire

    b. challenge

    c. reject

    d. earn.

The committee met, discussed the subject, and then appointed Mr. Jefferson and me to make the **draft** of a **document** on independence, I suppose because we were the two first on the list.

---

13. *Draft* most nearly means
    a. beginning

    b. attempt

    c. title

    d. appearance.

14. *Document* most nearly means
    a. testament

    b. proof

    c. paper

    d. certificate.

Reason first, Mr. Jefferson, you are a Virginian, and a Virginian ought to appear at the head of this **business**.

---

15. *Business* most nearly means
    a. time

    b. committee

c. group

d. task.

Reason second, I am **obnoxious**, suspected, and unpopular, but you are very much **otherwise**.

----

16. *Obnoxious* most nearly means
   a. objectionable

   b. unpleasant

   c. disgusting

   d. foul.

17. *Otherwise* most nearly means
   a. admired

   b. similar

   c. unpleasant

   d. opposite.

When you have **drawn** it up, we will have a meeting.

----

18. *Drawn* most nearly means
   a. brought

   b. written

c. tied

d. planned.

As you now know, when John Adams asked Thomas Jefferson to write the "Declaration of Independence," Jefferson responded, "I will do as well as I can." He certainly did, composing a masterpiece of literary and political power, one of the country's and the world's most famous public documents.

ACTIVITY 3: CREATING QUICKSHOTS

What summer holiday features cookouts, parades, picnics, and fireworks to celebrate America's birthday? If you guessed the Fourth of July, you're right. Following is the birth announcement of America, the famous opening of Thomas Jefferson's Declaration of Independence. Using an online or offline dictionary, jot down a one-word quickshot for each of the bolded words. Be sure that the synonym you choose fits the context of the sentence.

Here is the opening of Jefferson's document, with examples of a good quickshot and a bad quickshot.

EXAMPLES

Bad Quickshot: We hold these truths to be **self-evident** [*correct*].

Good Quickshot: We hold these truths to be **self-evident** [*obvious*].

Explanation: Jefferson means that the ideas he presents in the Declaration of Independence are obviously true. Only the second quickshot *fully* matches Jefferson's intended meaning.

From "Declaration of Independence"
by Thomas Jefferson, July 4, 1776

We hold these truths to be self-evident: that all men are created equal; that they are (1) **endowed** by their (2) **Creator** with certain (3) **unalienable** rights; that among these are life, (4) **liberty**, and the (5) **pursuit** of happiness; that to (6) **secure** these rights, governments are (7) **instituted** among men, (8) **deriving** their just powers from the (9) **consent** of the governed; that whenever any form of government becomes destructive of these (10) **ends**, it is the right of the people to (11) **alter** or to (12) **abolish** it, and to (13) **institute** new government, laying its (14) **foundation** on such principles and organizing its powers in such form as to them shall seem most likely to (15) **effect** their safety and happiness.

Wow! That's one super-long sentence, but what a memorable sentence it is! Jefferson certainly knew how to compose a sentence.

YOUR TURN: QUICKSHOT SENTENCES

Learning new words from quickshots deepens your reading but also strengthens your writing. Write ten sentences that include any ten of those quickshots from this section. To find them quickly, look for bolded words. They are the quickshots. Be sure each sentence clearly indicates you know the meaning of the word by providing a sufficient context. Study this example.

EXAMPLE

reviled [*disliked*]

Insufficient Context—The idea was reviled by the committee. *Because the sentence has insufficient context, the word reviled could mean almost anything—liked, accepted, praised, rejected, cheered,* and so forth.

Sufficient Context—Because the committee considered the proposal far too expensive, the idea was obviously reviled and rejected by majority vote after the presentation. *Because the sentence includes sufficient context through details about the expense of the proposed idea and therefore its rejection by the committee, the meaning of* reviled *is narrowed and focused.*

QUICKSHOTS IN THIS WORKTEXT

In the rest of *Nonfiction for Middle School: A Sentence-Composing Approach*, if a word might be a stumbling block, you'll have a quickshot definition to get you moving again, unlock the word's meaning, and help you understand the sentence.

Benjamin Franklin said this: "A word to the wise is **sufficient** [*enough*]." Ben never heard of quickshots, but he'd like them. Informed about quickshots, he might say this: "To be wise, learn quickshots." Why? Simple answer: The more words you know, the better you understand.

- -

*Words should be **acquired** [learned] because we*
urgently [desperately] *need them—to convey,*
to reach, to express something within us,
and to understand others.

—Vanna Bonta

- -

NONFICTION: WORDS FROM REAL LIFE

All of the excerpts in this worktext are *nonfiction*, the branch of literature that is not fiction, poetry, or drama. That's what nonfiction is not, but what is it?

NONFICTION DEFINED

Nonfiction is writing that's about what's real. Unlike fiction, none is made up. There are many kinds of nonfiction, including these:

- real people (biography)
- real thoughts (essays)
- real information (articles in magazines and newspapers, print or digital)
- real current events (news and journalism)
- real past events (history)
- real facts, processes, wikis, and blogs (information)
- real opinions about how good—or bad—things are (reviews)
- real memories (memoirs)
- real famous words (famous quotes, public documents, speeches)
- real memorable correspondence (letters)
- real education or instruction (textbooks, manuals, how-tos).

TRUE VS. FICTIONAL STORIES

Fiction is any story, short or long (novel), mostly from the author's imagination. Its source is the head of the author, not the history of an event (journalism) nor the facts of a real person's life (biography) nor the ideas of a person (essay) nor any other kind of nonfiction.

A fictional story never really happened except in the author's imagination. Think Harry Potter.

A nonfictional story did really happen and is based upon fact. Think Harry Truman, American two-term president from 1945 to 1953, whose biography *Truman* by David McCollough is a nonfiction account of Harry Truman's life.

Another difference is that nonfiction is based upon reality; fiction, upon make-believe. Harry Potter, in actuality, couldn't fly on a broomstick during Quidditch; however, in make-believe, through the skill and creativity of author J. K. Rowling (and through C.G.I. in the movie versions), Harry appears to be actually flying during Quidditch matches in the wizardly world at Hogwarts. Because of Rowling's skill in creating its realistic details, the flying seems to be actual—but isn't.

In actuality, though, President Harry Truman did order the first and only military use of an atomic bomb to speed the end of World War II. The bombing actually happened on August 6 in the city of Hiroshima, Japan, and August 9, 1945 in Nagasaki, Japan. The true story of one of those two cities is a nonfiction book titled *Hiroshima* by John Hersey, who went to that city, interviewed six survivors, and reported their experiences, observations.

The main difference between fiction and nonfiction is that fiction reflects scenes from an author's imagination, while nonfiction reflects events from an author's research, investigation, and discovery.

Much nonfiction, like most fiction, tells stories—real narratives of actual events (history or current events), or of real people (biography). Nonfiction authors try to tell those narratives truthfully, factually, to reflect accurately the event or the person they chronicle.

Other kinds of nonfiction tell the actuality of thought or procedure. Speeches or letters reveal the thoughts of the speaker or writer. Essays or articles or reviews reveal the opinion of the author.

In *Nonfiction for Middle School: A Sentence-Composing Approach*, you'll analyze nonfiction of various types by hundreds of authors—usually excerpts of sentences or paragraphs. Some are from biographies, some from essays, some from journalism articles, some from informational texts, some from public documents or speeches, some from stories of actual events or lives of real people.

ACTIVITY 1: FICTION OR NONFICTION?

Listed randomly are landmark titles of fiction and nonfiction known to culturally literate readers. Write *F* for fiction, *NF* for nonfiction. If you aren't sure, research the title to find out.

1. *In the Kingdom of Ice* Hampton Sides	**11.** *I Know Why the Caged Bird Sings* Maya Angelou
2. *Flowers for Algernon* Daniel Keyes	**12.** *Black Boy* Richard Wright
3. *Lord of the Flies* William Golding	**13.** *Looking for Alaska* John Green
4. *The Road Not Taken* Robert Frost	**14.** *A Raisin in the Sun* Lorraine Hansberry
5. *Romeo and Juliet* William Shakespeare	**15.** *The Story of My Life* Helen Keller
6. *Into the Wild* Jon Krakauer	**16.** *Go Ask Alice* Beatrice Sparks
7. Declaration of Independence Thomas Jefferson	**17.** *Unbroken* Laura Hillenbrand
8. *I Am Malala* Malala Yousafzai	**18.** *Night* Elie Wiesel
9. *The Hunger Games* Suzanne Collins	**19.** *Divergent* Veronica Roth
10. *Walden* Henry David Thoreau	**20.** *The Fault in Our Stars* John Green

NONFICTION TOPICS

What topics are subjects of nonfiction? Count the number of grains of sand in all the deserts of the Earth, and then count the number of drops of water in all the oceans on the planet, and then multiply both figures by a billion trillion. That's how many topics nonfiction has been written about—from *A* to *Z*, from common subjects (cars, travel, sports, health, friendship, money, and a billion more) to complex subjects (metaphysics, astrobiology, mycology, phylogeny, ontogeny, postmodernism, and a billion more).

A popular category of nonfiction is how-to books. On the Internet, amazon.com lists over 600,000 titles beginning with *How to*. Here are only a few of probably millions of such books:

- *How to Train a Wild Elephant* by Jan Chozen Bays
- *How to Babysit a Grandpa* by Jean Reagan and Lee Wildish
- *How to Cook Everything* by Mark Bittman
- *How to Be Photogenic: A Guide for Girls and Guys to Look Better in Pictures!* by F. Saeyang
- *How to Be Interesting* (In 10 Simple Steps) by Jessica Hagy
- *How to Talk So Kids Will Listen & Listen So Kids Will Talk* by Adele Faber and Elaine Mazlish
- *How to Raise the Perfect Dog: Through Puppyhood and Beyond* by Cesar Millan
- *How to Build a Fire: And Other Handy Things Your Grandfather Knew* by Erin Bried
- *How to Write a Book This Weekend, Even If You Flunked English Like I Did* by Vic Johnson

In *Nonfiction for Middle School: A Sentence-Composing Approach*, you'll read just a tiny bit of varied nonfiction, but through the activities, you'll increase your ability to read more deeply and write nonfiction more skillfully. (None will assign you to write a book over the weekend. Promise.)

IMPORTANCE OF NONFICTION

Why learn how to read and write nonfiction? Something done frequently should be something done well. Nonfiction is the kind of writing you'll probably read most often in college or the workplace. In college, students read textbooks, print and digital, in almost all courses, and they are expected to master the contents on their own—scientific data, mathematical theories, psychology studies, anthropological research reports, and many others. At work, employees often are required to read database information, operational and procedural manuals, product descriptions and inventories, focus group summaries evaluating products and services, comparative market statistics, and much more. A lot of that nonfiction is challenging, requiring advanced skills of interpreting for reading, and composing for writing.

Beyond college or career, many people simply enjoy reading nonfiction for entertainment, information, or recreation, sometimes preferring it over fiction.

The purpose of this worktext is to help you become a better reader and writer of any nonfiction, including kinds requiring deep reading.

Force yourself to reflect on what you read, sentence by sentence, and paragraph by paragraph.

—Samuel Taylor Coleridge

UBER-LITERACY

By focusing on nonfiction sentences and paragraphs—how they are built and how they convey meaning—this worktext, *Nonfiction for Middle School: A Sentence-Composing Approach*, promotes uber-literacy, the kind of deep reading that characterizes skillful readers. Carefully completing activities in this worktext, you can become not just literate. You can become uber-literate. Just so you know, the prefix *uber-* means "very."

Reading is to the mind what exercise is to the body.

—Richard Steele

YOUR TURN: SUMMARIZING

A good way to learn something is to teach it. That's because to teach requires understanding of the topic taught.

Pretend your classmate had to miss school during the time your class learned about nonfiction presented in this section **NONFICTION: WORDS FROM REAL LIFE.** Your classmate sent you a text or email asking you to summarize what the class learned about nonfiction versus fiction.

Write a summary of what you learned about nonfiction to send to your friend so she or he can keep up with the class and not fall behind.

Even though this situation is fictitious, you will benefit because you'll be acting like a teacher, strengthening what you know about nonfiction. Often teachers themselves learn more deeply what is taught to their students.

Directions: After reviewing the information in this section, do the following to prepare a good summary of what's there.

1. Review the information about nonfiction in this section.

2. Explain the differences between nonfiction and fiction.

3. List and explain important terms and categories of nonfiction for an absentee.

4. Explain benefits of reading nonfiction.

5. Draft your summary, including information about nonfiction terms, types, and benefits.

6. Include your best sentence and paragraph style, so good that your summary could be published as an example of excellent student writing (or maybe tacked on your teacher's bulletin board).

7. Exchange your draft with other students in your class for suggestions to improve your summary of nonfiction, and give them suggestions, too. Then revise several times until your summary is finished.

When you finish, congratulations! You've learned—and taught—a lot about nonfiction, and you are ready to move on in this worktext to deepen your knowledge and skill in reading and writing nonfiction.

When a nonfiction sentence is composed, it is intended to be read. Sometimes, though, especially with challenging nonfiction, what's written is not read *well*, and so the writer's intention isn't fully met. Comprehension and communication are incomplete.

To understand a challenging sentence fully requires getting into the head of the writer to export meaning, then importing that meaning into your own head, without losing, distorting, or ignoring any of the writer's meaning.

In *Nonfiction for Middle School: A Sentence-Composing Approach*, you'll learn and practice skills to read and write nonfiction well. The method breaks down reading and writing nonfiction to a basic unit of meaning—the sentence. Sentence activities in this worktext increase your skill in reading and writing nonfiction for use in and beyond middle school.

SPEAKING AND WRITING: DIFFERENCES

Spoken sentences are usually short, simple, with easy words. Each sentence is basic in what it says and how it says it. Spoken sentences are quick and easy to understand.

Written sentences in nonfiction are often long, intricately built, with more demanding vocabulary. In addition to a subject and a predicate, most are packed with other sentence parts, requiring deep, slow reading for full understanding.

ACTIVITY: SPOKEN VERSUS WRITTEN SENTENCES

Below are some nonfiction sentences, then a translation of each into a series of spoken sentences. As you will see, the written version is harder to understand than the spoken version.

1a. *Writing:* Dotted with sticker bushes, tumbleweed, and coiled rattlesnakes, the desert around our house seems to have no reason for existence, other than providing a place for people to dump things they no longer want, like tires and mattresses.

Andre Agassi, *Open: An Autobiography*

1b. *Speaking:* We live in a desert. It is dotted with sticker bushes. There's tumbleweeds here and there. There's even rattlesnakes coiled up. The desert seems kind of useless. The only thing people use it for is a dumping ground. They throw stuff there they don't want, like tires and mattresses.

2a. *Writing:* One structure, rejected at first as a monstrosity, became the World Fair's **emblem** [*symbol*], a machine huge and terrifying, **eclipsing** [*overshadowing*] instantly the tower of Alexandre Eiffel that had so wounded America's pride.

Erik Larson, *The Devil in the White City*

2b. *Speaking:* One structure was rejected. It was considered at first a monstrosity. The structure was a machine, which was huge and terrifying. It outdid the French Eiffel tower that had hurt the pride of America.

3a. *Writing:* As the contest for the State Legislature that would name his successor raged in Missouri, Senator Benton stood fast by his **post** [*position*] in Washington, outspoken to the end in his condemnation of the views his **constituents** [*voters*] now embraced.

John F. Kennedy, *Profiles in Courage*

3b. *Speaking:* Senator Benton never changed his mind. He even voiced opinions that sharply disagreed with the people who elected him. He continued to express those strong views during the battle in Missouri among the candidates who were fighting to replace him as senator.

Throughout this worktext, you'll sample nonfiction sentences that illustrate strong writing and apply what you learn to building better sentences like those of authors. Their sentences are the focus of upcoming activities to deepen your ability to read and write nonfiction.

YOUR TURN: CONTRASTING WRITING AND SPEAKING

Duplicate the previous activity (pp. 24–25) by converting each nonfiction sentence below into a series of spoken sentences.

EXAMPLE

Writing: When I was eleven years old, in the summer of 1996, I was getting ready to enter middle school and the sixth grade.
          Peter Nelson and Hunter Scott, *Left for Dead*

Speaking: It happened when I was eleven. It was summertime. It was the year 1996. Then I was about to go to middle school. I would be in the sixth grade.

Comments: The written version says everything in just one sentence; the spoken version, five sentences. The written version has sentence-composing tools—*when I was eleven years old and in the summer of 1966*; the spoken version, no tools. The written version is concise; the spoken version, wordy.

1. When I was about 19, I had a girlfriend, Ros, whose father was a slightly **forbidding** [*stern*] headmaster, a big **gruff** [*grouchy*] bear of a man.

   Alan Rusbridger, *Play It Again*

2. In a recent two-and-a-half-year period, **corporate** [*business*] profits surged 87 percent, while wages rose just 4.5 percent.

   Studs Terkel, *Working*

3. Like many joyful souls, my friend laughed hardest at someone else's jokes, with a wide-open, belly-shaking laugh that never failed to lift me out of whatever spiritual **doldrums** [*blues*] I was **navigating** [*experiencing*].

   James Martin, *Between Heaven and Mirth*

4. My father's **theory** [*belief*], a treatment all his pre-born children received, was that if the eye of their pregnant mother was constantly observing the beauty of nature, this beauty would somehow become **transmitted** [*sent*] to the mind of the unborn baby within its mother's womb, causing that baby to grow up to be a lover of beautiful things.

   Roald Dahl, *Boy* (adapted)

5. On January 15, 1919, a huge tank of molasses, 50 feet high, burst open at Boston's Purity Distilling Company, **spewing** [*pouring*] more than two million gallons of molasses out into the street, with waves 10 feet high rushing down the street at more than 30 miles per hour, swallowing and killing people, and knocking buildings off their foundations.

   Marc Aronson and HP Newquist, *Boys Only*

MIRROR IMAGES: IMITATING NONFICTION SENTENCES

Because nonfiction sentences are very different from the sentences we speak, learning how to read and write those sentences is very important to improve your reading and writing. This section, imitating model sentences and paragraphs from nonfiction sources, will show you how.

My entire writing career fueled itself with
*the **mimicry** [imitation] of sentences*
of the great writers I loved the best.

Pat Conroy, *My Reading Life*

The building blocks of nonfiction, sentences are a good place to start learning how authors write. Imitating their methods will help you build sentences like theirs.

ACTIVITY 1: IDENTIFYING MEANINGFUL SENTENCE PARTS

Identify the sentence divided into sentence parts that make sense.

1a. I looked with / a mixture of admiration and awe at / Peter, a boy who could and did imitate /a police siren every / morning on his way to the / showers.

1b. I looked / with a mixture of admiration / and awe at Peter, / a boy who could and did imitate a police siren / every morning / on his way to the showers.

Robert Russell, *To Catch an Angel*

2a. Gimble the chimpanzee / started leaping about in the tree / tops, swinging vigorously from / one branch to the next, climbing up then / jumping down to catch himself on a / bough below.

2b. Gimble the chimpanzee / started leaping about / in the tree tops, swinging vigorously / from one branch to the next, climbing up / then jumping down to catch himself / on a bough below.

Jane Goodall, Through a Window

3a. Contrary to / popular / impressions, leprosy is not highly / contagious.

3b. Contrary / to popular impressions, / leprosy is not / highly contagious.

Norman Cousins, Anatomy of an Illness

4a. Robert dove deep / into chemistry and physics in high school, / graduated from Harvard University in 1925, / then earned advanced degrees at top universities / in Britain and Germany.

4b. Robert dove deep into / chemistry and physics in high school, / graduated from Harvard / University in 1925, then earned advanced / degrees at top universities in Britain and / Germany.

Steve Sheinkin, Bomb

5a. Back in / London, the ship had been / visited by two officers from Scotland / Yard, patrolling the wharves in / hopes of **thwarting** [*preventing*] the / couple's escape.

5b. Back in London, / the ship had been visited / by two officers from Scotland Yard, / patrolling the wharves / in hopes / of thwarting the couple's escape.

Erik Larson, Thunderstruck

ACTIVITY 2: CHUNKING SENTENCE IMITATIONS

Copy the model and the one sentence in the pair that imitates it. Chunk the model and its imitation into equivalent sentence parts.

EXAMPLE

Model Sentence: For several days, Henrietta's corpse lay in the hallway of the house, doors propped open at each end to let in the cool wet breeze that would keep her body fresh.

Rebecca Skloot, *The Immortal Life of Henrietta Lack*

a. After the paint finally dried on the wicker chair, the paint can sat in the sun outside the shed, and its lid was closed tight so that the paint inside wouldn't dry out.

b. With only a dollar, Ryan's wallet sat on the counter of the cashier, his pockets both searched to find in at least one some coins that would supply the balance.

Imitation Sentence: b

Meaningful Chunks: (The number and placement of chunks may vary. Here is one possibility.)

1. For several days, / Henrietta's corpse lay / in the hallway of the house, / doors propped open at each end / to let in the cool wet breeze / that would keep her body fresh.

2. With only a dollar, / Tenell's wallet sat / on the counter of the cashier, / his pockets both searched / to find in at least one some coins / that would supply the remaining balance.

1. **Model Sentence:** Mom, in an unnaturally calm voice, explained what had happened and asked if we could have a ride to the hospital.

Jeanette Walls, *The Glass Castle*

a. Darlene, at an annoyingly rapid pace, described what they had said and explained that she could no longer put up with that behavior.

b. Frank, hoping not to be overheard by anyone, yelled to his sister about what was happening in the kitchen after they ate.

2. **Model Sentence:** On her monthly visits, dressed in stylish **vintage** [old] furs, diamonds, and spike heels, which constantly caught between loose floorboards, she forced smiles and held her tongue.

Maya Angelou, The Heart of a Woman

    a. In his comfortable car, dressed in denim blue jeans, flannels, and tennis shoes, which frequently drummed on the gray floor mats, he hummed tunes and watched the traffic.

    b. In late afternoons, thinking about the chores that had been completed and those still left to do, which bothered him, he tried to enjoy the beautiful weather in spite of his obligations.

3. **Model Sentence:** Anne Frank, who was thirteen when she began her diary and fifteen when she was forced to stop, wrote without **reserve** [*shyness*] about her likes and dislikes.

Otto H. Frank and Mirjam Pressler (editors),
The Diary of Anne Frank

    a. Benjamin Franklin, a famous American inventor and interesting historical figure, is credited with flying the kite that led to the discovery of electricity.

    b. Jane Eyre, who was a child when the novel of her name began and nineteen when she was able to marry, spoke with honesty about her likes and experiences.

4. **Model Sentence:** The *Carpathia*'s ship's passengers pitched in **gallantly** [*unselfishly*] to help the survivors of the *Titanic*, providing extra toothbrushes, lending clothes, sewing smocks for the children out of steamer blankets brought along in the lifeboats.

Walter Lord, A Night to Remember

    a. Neighboring states near New Orleans worked **diligently** [*hard*] to provide relief to the victims of Hurricane Katrina, establishing relief centers, providing food, giving water to the victims out of clean supplies ferried in from nearby reservoirs.

b. The neighbors of the burned-out village wanted to help those who had survived by sharing with them what food, clothing, and supplies they were able to **accumulate** [*gather*] from donations and from stores, which provided free baby supplies.

5. **Model Sentence:** Lincoln knew that many citizens of the North had lost their stomach for this war, with its modern technology like repeating rifles and long-range artillery that have brought about staggering losses of life.

Bill O'Reilly and Martin Dugard, Killing Lincoln

a. Jeff Bezos, **entrepreneur** [*businessman*] and **innovator** [*inventor*], changed the way people shop, including online, through making many products like books, music, videos, even clothes and shoes, available with one-click shopping.

b. Steve Jobs realized that many people in the world had raised their interest in his products, with their amazing innovations like iTunes and iPhones that have made happen incredible advances in technology.

ACTIVITY 3: MATCHING

Match the imitation with the model it imitates.

Model Sentences	Imitations
1. While everyone scattered, I crept into my favorite hiding place, the little closet tucked under the stairs. Jean Fritz, *Homesick: My Own Story*	**a.** The sound of string guitar, the most important instrument in the band, was suddenly throbbing and harmonizing with the singer.

2. Still in pajamas, Harry Gold raced around his cluttered bedroom, pulling out desk drawers, tossing boxes out of the closet, and yanking books from the shelves.

> Steve Sheinkin, *Bomb*

3. The first gray light had just appeared in the living room windows, black mirrors a moment ago, now opening on the view of the woods to the south.

> Tracy Kidder, *Old Friends*

4. When I went out to my woodpile, I observed two large ants, the one red, the other much larger, fiercely **contending** [*fighting*] with one another.

> Henry David Thoreau, *Walden*

5. The face of Liliana Methol, the fifth woman in the plane, was badly bruised and covered with blood.

> Piers Paul Read, *Alive*

b. Never without advisors, FDR moved to the Oval Office, asking for honest reaction, watching faces in the inner circle, and shuffling papers around his desk.

c. After he went over the accounting figures, he saw several disturbing problems, the one careless, the other obviously planned, undoubtedly pointing toward illegal activity.

d. When the rain ended, Levar came out from the shelter, a temporary tent made from a cardboard box.

e. The last night sounds had just faded amid the small town shops, stores alive until then, now shutting down the commerce of the businesses in the town.

Only through imitation do we develop toward originality.

—John Steinbeck, *Travels with Charley in Search of America*

ACTIVITY 4: IMITATING SENTENCES OF AUTHORS

Write an imitation of the model sentence, building your sentence like the model by writing similar sentence parts. In your imitation sentence—after learning more online or offline about your topic—tell information your readers might not know about any of these topics: culture, entertainment, health, history, inventions, literature, media, politics, religion, science, space, sports, technology, transportation, or some other interesting topic.

EXAMPLE

Model: Jackie Robinson's complex fate was to be the first black player in the major leagues of baseball in America in the twentieth century.

Arnold Rampersad, *Jackie Robinson: A Biography*

Sample Imitation: Elvis Presley's **toxic** [*poisonous*] destiny was to be the most recognizable superstar in the entertainment world with zero chance of privacy.

---

1. **Model:** He fell back, exhausted, his ankle pounding.

   Ralph Ellison, "Flying Home"

Sample Imitation: Florence Griffith Joyner stood up, triumphant, her victory **assured** [guaranteed].

2. **Model:** He lived alone, a **gaunt** [*thin*], stooped figure who wore a heavy black overcoat and a misshapen **fedora** [*hat*] on those rare occasions when he left his apartment.

   Barack Obama, *Dreams from My Father*

Sample Imitation: Harper Lee lived **frugally** [*thriftily*], a small intense woman who shared an undying literary interest and a burning ambition with her few friends after her arrival in New York City.

3. **Model:** In his room on the ground floor, to the right of the front door, Father Kleinsorge changed into a military uniform, which he had **acquired** [*gotten*] when he was teaching at the school in Kobe and which he wore during air-raid alerts.

   John Hersey, *Hiroshima*

Sample Imitation: On the way to the fire drill, outside the school's main entrance, high school teachers recorded the presence of students, which they had been instructed to do when there was any emergency drill at school and which they took very seriously when emergencies arose.

4. **Model:** Concerned with her father, who lay dying in the bedroom, but not wanting to miss the moon landing, Phyllis was with her father when her mother called her to come and see Neil Armstrong set foot on the moon.

Frank McCourt, Teacher Man

Sample Imitation: Awarded the Nobel Prize for literature, which seldom has been given to a female writer, and publishing only story collections and one novel, Alice Munro was not at home when the Awards Committee called her to announce the prize and congratulate her on her achievement.

5. **Model:** Seventeenth century European women and men sometimes wore beauty patches in the shape of hearts, suns, moons, and stars, applying them to their breasts and faces, to draw an admirer's eye away from any **imperfections** [*blemishes*], which, in that era, too often included smallpox scars.

Diane Ackerman, "The Face of Beauty"

Sample Imitation: Twenty-first century women and men often wore elaborate tattoos in the shape of animals, scripture, people, and sayings, displaying them on any part of their bodies, to make a comment on their lifestyles, which, in this time, very often included **discretionary** [*additional*] income.

YOUR TURN: IMITATING WITHIN A PARAGRAPH

Research a famous battle to write an informational paragraph that includes some sentences based on models.

WRITING PROCESS

Researching: Learn online or offline about an important battle. Some possibilities include these battles, or choose a more recent battle of historical significance:

Battle	Where and When
Hastings	England, 1066
Lexington & Concord	Massachusetts, 1775
Waterloo	Belgium, 1815
Gettysburg	Pennsylvania, 1863
Guadalcanal	SW Pacific, 1942–43
Tet Offensive	South Vietnam, 1968

Prewriting: From your research, list facts and details of that battle, including the outcome and historical significance of the battle.

Drafting: Draft a paragraph with information about that battle.

Refining and Revising: Choose *three* of the model sentences below to imitate within your paragraph, using their structure but describing your chosen battle.

MODEL SENTENCES from Steven Kroll's book *By the Dawn's Early Light* about the history of the national anthem "Star-Spangled Banner." Choose three to imitate and include in your paragraph.

1. On June 18, a poorly prepared United States declared war on Great Britain, and for almost two years there were battles on land and sea.

2. Between the 19th and 25th of August, 1814, British troops defeated the inexperienced American militia at Bladensburg, Maryland, burned a defenseless Washington, and returned to their ships to head for Baltimore.

3. At Fort McHenry in Baltimore, the Fort's storm flag, measuring twenty-five by seventeen feet, was flying during the battle.

4. The larger flag, the Fort's garrison flag, was raised in victory celebration as Francis Scott Key, composer of "The Star-Spangled Banner," sailed back to Baltimore.

5. With the collapse of the assault on Baltimore, a peace treaty was signed on December 24, 1814.

Peer Responding: Exchange your draft with other students in your class for suggestions to improve your paragraph, and give them suggestions, too. Then revise until your paragraph is finished.

Creating a Title: Create a memorable title and subtitle, with a colon between them. *Example:* "The Battle at Fort McHenry: A Victory Song for the Nation."

SENTENCE TOOLS: OPENERS, S-V SPLITS, CLOSERS

Sentence-composing tools are parts within a sentence that add dazzle and detail. They are movable within a sentence, just like furniture in your room.

Your bed in your room isn't nailed to the floor, right? Well, neither are tools glued to just one place in a sentence. Just as you can move your bed around the room to find a better place, authors can move sentence parts within a sentence to place them more effectively.

Usually, within your room, the bed can be moved to a couple of places. Within sentences, you also have just three choices to place sentence-composing tools: *opener, S-V split, closer*.

Openers are placed before the subject of a sentence; S-V splits, between the subject and its verb; closers, after the predicate of a sentence.

Authors use all three positions. You can, too. Next, you'll learn and practice how they do it. It's a good thing to know how to move things around to put them in better places, including sentence-composing tools.

Below are examples of tools as openers, S-V splits, closers. The subject of the sentence is underlined <u>once</u>, the predicate <u>twice</u>. Tools are bolded.

EXAMPLES

The first sentence is *before* adding tools; the second is *after* adding tools, resulting in a more informative, varied, and interesting sentence.

On the Mark: Tools are punctuated with commas.

> ### Openers
> **1a.** *Before:* <u>Sergeant Fales</u> <u>felt anger with the pain.</u>
>
> **1b.** *After:* **A big broad-faced man who had fought in Panama and during the Gulf War,** Sergeant Fales felt anger with the pain.
>
> Mark Bowden, *Black Hawk Down*

2a. *Before:* He <u>stopped his rig on the crest of a low rise</u>.

2b. *After:* **Worried that he would get stuck in the snow if he drove farther**, he stopped his rig on the crest of a low rise.

> Jon Krakauer, *Into the Wild*

3a. *Before:* Hitler's planes, tanks, and soldiers <u>slashed deep into Polish territory</u>.

3b. *After:* **Using a new style of attack known as blitzkrieg, German for *lightning war***, Hitler's planes, tanks, and soldiers slashed deep into Polish territory.

> Steve Sheinkin, *Bomb*

4a. *Before:* The smell of burned flesh <u>hit Pete even before the hatch was completely open</u>.

4b. *After:* **As the helicopter came down between the pine trees and settled onto the bogs where the accident had occurred**, the smell of burned flesh hit Pete even before the hatch was completely open.

> Tom Wolfe, *The Right Stuff*

5a. *Before:* The Italians <u>saw sea planes as the way of the future</u>.

5b. *After:* **While the American fliers were investing all their energies in land planes**, the Italians saw sea planes as the way of the future.

> Bill Bryson, *One Summer*

S-V Splits

6a. *Before:* Talloi <u>asked why they were back</u>.

6b. *After:* Talloi, **breathing hard and speaking slowly**, asked why they were back.

> Ishmael Beah, *A Long Way Gone*

7a. *Before:* Arrowhead crabs have eyes set so far apart they can see in almost a complete circle.

7b. *After:* Arrowhead crabs, **bright spiderlike reef creatures familiar to scuba-divers,** have eyes set so far apart they can see in almost a complete circle.

Diane Ackerman, A Natural History of the Senses

8a. *Before:* Nancy Gunter came to work before midnight.

8b. *After:* Nancy Gunter, **who was in charge of the astronaut crew quarters in the operations and checkout building,** came to work before midnight.

Hugh Harris, Challenger

9a. *Before:* A thousand pages was an unwieldy load requiring both arms to carry.

9b. *After:* A thousand pages, **loosely bound and with no two sheets quite matching,** was an unwieldy load requiring both arms to carry.

Bill Bryson, Shakespeare

10a. *Before:* Chung launched a project in South Florida to represent mentally incompetent immigrants facing deportation.

10b. *After:* Chung, **the daughter of South Korean immigrants and a passionate advocate for human rights,** launched a project in South Florida to represent mentally incompetent immigrants facing deportation.

Sonia Nazario, Enrique's Journey

Closers

11a. *Before:* My mother had been scolding me.

11b. *After:* My mother had been scolding me, **telling me to keep still, warning me that I must make no noise**.

Richard Wright, Black Boy

12a. *Before:* Sharks glided in lazy loops around their rafts.

12b. *After:* Sharks glided in lazy loops around their rafts, **dragging their backs along the rafts, waiting**.

Laura Hillenbrand, Unbroken

13a. *Before:* The town's natives did their shopping on King Street.

13b. *After:* The town's natives did their shopping on King Street, **the town's shopping strip, a slice of chain department stores, auto dealerships, fast-food restaurants**.

Tracy Kidder, Home Town

14a. *Before:* She was an accomplished violinist.

14b. *After:* She was an accomplished violinist, **far out of the ordinary in fact, her talent so highly valued in her home that growing up she never had to do the dishes for fear that her fingers would be damaged by soap and water**.

Daniel James Brown, The Boys in the Boat

15a. *Before:* The pilot was busy.

15b. *After:* The pilot was busy, **trying to restart the engine, working to raise somebody on the radio, reviewing emergency procedures, keeping the right glide angle to hold the plane in the air as long as possible and yet**

maintain flying speed, trying all the while to locate a place suitable for an emergency landing.

Gary Paulsen, *Guts*

Mixes

16a. *Before:* Clarkston was sometimes called Goatsville.

16b. *After:* Clarkston, **in the years after the Civil War**, was sometimes called Goatsville, **perhaps because goats were used to keep grass low by the train tracks**. (*S-V split, closer*)

Warren St. John, *Outcasts United: A Refugee Team, an American Town*

17a. *Before:* Time stood still throughout the world.

17b. *After:* **At 9:32 a.m. on July 16, 1969,** time stood still throughout the world, **as thousands converged on the Kennedy Space Center and millions tuned in on live television to watch Apollo 11's launch to the moon.** (*opener, closer*)

Charles River Editors,
Apollo 11: The History and Legacy of the First Moon Landing

18a. *Before:* None of my dogs ever got killed by moose.

18b. *After:* **Though I was attacked or had dangerous encounters many more times,** none of my dogs ever got killed by moose, **though I knew of other racers who lost dogs that way either in training or during the Iditarod race.** (*opener, closer*)

Gary Paulsen, *Guts*

19a. *Before:* We came to a damp little shut-up town.

19b. *After:* **After forty years in the painful wet desert with no cloud by day nor pillar of fire by night to guide us,** we came to a damp little shut-up town, **whose name escapes me because I never learned it**. (*opener, closer*)

John Steinbeck, *Travels with Charley in Search of America*

20a. *Before:* The *Tigress* was pushing through the loose floes and icebergs off the coast of Labrador.

20b. *After:* **On a misty morning in late April 1873**, the *Tigress*, **a steam ship out of Conception Bay, Newfoundland**, was pushing through the loose floes and icebergs off the coast of Labrador, **heading for the seasonal seal-hunting grounds**. (*opener, S-V split, closer*)

Hampton Sides, *In the Kingdom of Ice*

Obviously, filling those three positions with sentence-composing tools helps you build better sentences, thick not thin, long not short, packed not empty, in and beyond middle school.

You'll never get anywhere with all those damn little short sentences.

—Gregory Clark, *A Social Perspective on the Function of Writing*

For reading and writing nonfiction, knowledge of sentence structure—which means how sentences are built—is crucial. Perhaps the most important aspect of sentence structure is kinds of sentence parts used by writers as tools to build better sentences. Good writers of nonfiction and almost every other kind of writing use various sentence tools to build better sentences with greater detail, information, style, and power.

To illustrate the importance of such sentence tools, here is a paragraph presented twice: without tools, then with tools.

BACKGROUND: The book *Unbroken* by Laura Hillenbrand, a compellingly interesting nonfiction account, chronicles the survival of Louis

Zamperini and two other members of the American Army Air Force crew adrift in the Pacific Ocean in two rubber rafts after their plane had been shot down during World War II in June 1943. Formerly one of the fastest runners in the Olympics, Zamperini against all hope manages to survive.

In the excerpt below, from the preface to the book, the author describes the plight of Zamperini and the two others, who drift amid shark-infested waters for twenty-seven days, without food, their bodies sunburned and shrunken to skeletons. Without hope of rescue, they waste away, adrift for over one thousand miles, alone and engulfed in a million miles of the Pacific Ocean.

The excerpt recounts what at first seems to be a hope of rescue.

WITHOUT TOOLS (*140 words*)

(1) The men heard a distant, deep strumming. (2) Every airman knew that sound. (3) Their eyes caught a glint in the sky. (4) Zamperini, then shook powdered dye into the water. (5) The plane kept going. (6) The men sagged. (7) Then the sound returned. (8) The crew had seen them.

(9) The castaways waved and shouted. (10) The plane swept alongside the rafts. (11) Zamperini saw the profiles of the crewmen.

(12) The water seemed to boil. (13) It was machine gun fire. (14) This was not an American rescue plane. (15) It was a Japanese bomber.

(16) The men pitched themselves into the water and hung together under the rafts. (17) The firing blazed on. (18) The men climbed back onto the one raft that was still mostly inflated. (19) The bomber banked sideways. (20) Zamperini could see the muzzles of the machine guns. (21) Zamperini looked toward his crewmates. (22) Zamperini splashed overboard alone.

(23) The sharks were done waiting.

WITH TOOLS (*underlined*)

(283 words—twice the length of the excerpt without tools)

(1) On that morning of the twenty-seventh day, the men heard a distant, deep strumming. (2) Every airman knew that sound: pistons. (3) Their eyes caught a glint in the sky—a plane, high overhead. (4) Zamperini, firing two **flares** [*signals*], then shook powdered dye into the water, enveloping the rafts in a circle of vivid orange. (5) The plane kept going, slowly disappearing. (6) The men sagged. (7) Then the sound returned, the plane coming back into view. (8) The crew had seen them.

(9) With arms shrunken to little more than bone and yellowed skin, the castaways waved and shouted, their voices thin from thirst. (10) The plane, dropping low, swept alongside the rafts. (11) Zamperini saw the profiles of the crewmen, dark against bright blueness.

(12) With a terrific roaring sound, the water, and the rafts themselves, seemed to boil. (13) It was machine gun fire. (14) This was not an American rescue plane. (15) It was a Japanese bomber.

(16) The men pitched themselves into the water and hung together under the rafts, **cringing** [*cowering*] as bullets punched through the rubber and sliced **effervescent** [*shining*] lines in the water around their faces. (17) The firing blazed on, gradually sputtering out as the bomber overshot them. (18) The men, dragging themselves, climbed back onto the one raft that was still mostly inflated. (19) The bomber **banked** [*tilted*] sideways, circling toward them again. (20) As it leveled off, Zamperini could see the muzzles of the machine guns, aimed directly at them. (21) Zamperini looked toward his crewmates, too weak to go back in the water. (22) As they lay down on the floor of the raft, hands over their heads, Zamperini splashed overboard alone.

(23) Somewhere beneath him, the sharks were done waiting, bending their bodies in the water and swimming toward Zamperini, the man under the raft. (adapted)

In the excerpt from this nonfiction book, the sentence tools account for half of the original.

As you can see in the excerpt from *Unbroken*, an author varies the positions for the sentence tools: *opener* (at the beginning of a sentence); *S-V split* (between a subject and its verb); *closer* (at the end of a sentence). Within the excerpt are twenty-six sentence tools, adding detail, style, information, and power to the writing. Here are all of them, arranged by position:

OPENERS

- on that morning of the twenty-seventh day
- with arms shrunken to little more than bone and yellowed skin
- with a terrific roaring sound
- as it leveled off
- as they lay down on the floor of the raft
- hands over their heads
- somewhere beneath him

S-V SPLITS

- firing two flares
- dropping low
- and the rafts themselves
- dragging themselves

CLOSERS

- pistons
- a plane, high overhead
- enveloping the rafts in a circle of vivid orange

- slowly disappearing

- the plane coming back into view

- their voices thin from thirst

- dark against bright blueness

- cringing as bullets punched through the rubber and sliced effervescent lines in the water around their faces

- gradually sputtering out as the bomber overshot them

- circling toward them again

- aimed directly at them

- too weak to go back in the water

- bending their bodies in the water

- swimming toward Zamperini

- the man under the raft

Authors of nonfiction and other kinds of writing use all three positions within their sentences. You can, too. Next, you'll learn and practice how they do it, so that you can become a deeper reader and a better writer of nonfiction and every other kind of skillful writing.

> *For me the big chore is always the same: how to begin a sentence, how to continue it, how to complete it.*
>
> —Claude Simon, *winner of the Nobel Prize in literature*

Now, in the next sections of this worktext, you'll learn how to do exactly that by using tools in all three of those positions: *openers, S-V splits, closers.*

THE OPENER: GOOD BEGINNINGS

Sometimes good writers use sentence tools at the beginning of the sentence to provide up-front information because it's important. Take a look at sentences without tools up-front. Then contrast them with sentences with tools at the beginning called *openers* because they come at the beginning of the sentence.

An opener is a sentence tool at the beginning of a sentence followed by a comma.

1a. I came to philosophy as a last resort.

1b. A professional football player, print and television journalist, academic English teacher, and world-traveler, I came to philosophy as a last resort.

> John McMurty, "Kill 'Em! Crush 'Em! Eat 'Em Raw!"

2a. The bulk of the Californians were young Americans who had families back east.

2b. Although they came from different ports and different continents and by different routes, the **bulk** [*majority*] of the Californians were young Americans who had families back east.

> Stephen E. Ambrose, *Nothing Like It in the World*

3a. She forced smiles and held her tongue.

3b. On her monthly visits, dressed in stylish **vintage** [*old*] furs, diamonds, and spike heels, which constantly caught between loose floorboards, she forced smiles and held her tongue.

> Maya Angelou, *The Heart of a Woman*

ACTIVITY 1: MATCHING

Match the opener with its sentence. Write out each sentence, inserting the opener at the caret mark (^) and underlining it. **Punctuation:** Use a comma after each opener.

Sentence	Opener
1. ^ , we would reduce our country's oil **consumption** [*use*] by over 1.1 million barrels of oil every week. Barbara Kingsolver, *Animal, Vegetable, Miracle*	**a.** If, when you've finished reading a book, the pages are filled with your notes
2. ^ , I would have tried to talk her in off the ledge and maybe **placate** [*calm*] her with a goldfish. John Grogan, *Marley & Me*	**b.** Though he gave up professional performing at the age of thirty-five for a more **lucrative** [*profitable*] career as a design manager at a stereo company
3. ^ , you know that you read actively. Mortimer Adler, "How to Mark a Book"	**c.** If every U.S. citizen ate just one meal a week (any meal) composed of locally and organically raised meats and produce
4. ^ , his life and our home remained **saturated** [*filled*] with music. Perri Knize, *A Piano Odyssey*	**d.** When a seat in the state legislature opened up in 1996
5. ^ , some friends persuaded me to run for the office, and I won. Barack Obama, *Dreams from My Father*	**e.** If Jenny really only wanted a dog to hone her parenting skills

ACTIVITY 2: COMBINING

Combine each pair of sentences by making the underlined part *an opener* to insert at the caret mark (^). Write out the result—the author's original sentence. Use a comma after the opener.

EXAMPLE

Two Sentences: ^, Chicago is America's city, dreaming America's dream. Chicago is <u>an imperfect place</u>.

One Sentence with Opener: <u>An imperfect place</u>, Chicago is America's city, dreaming America's dream.

Alex Kotlowitz, Never a City So Real

1. ^ , Mr. Clutter had in large measure obtained it. He was <u>always certain of what he wanted from the world</u>.

Truman Capote, In Cold Blood

2. ^ , the revolutionaries had descended onto the streets in broad daylight. They were <u>no longer **specters** [*ghosts*] on rooftops, or disembodied howls in the dark</u>.

Roya Hakakian, Journey from the Land of No

3. ^ , he was setting out alone. He was <u>like many of the men in the Great Migration, and like many emigrants in general</u>.

Isabel Wilkerson, The Warmth of Other Suns

4. ^ , I gave myself up to the gentle warmth and thanked God that no matter what evil I had done in my life He had allowed me to live to see this day. I was <u>in my robe and barefoot in the backyard, under cover of going to see about my new beans</u>.

Maya Angelou, I Know Why the Caged Bird Sings

5. ^ , the Somali Bantu minority had undergone more than three hundred years of almost uninterrupted **persecution** [*attack*]. They are <u>an assemblage of agricultural tribes from the area of East Africa now **comprising** [*including*] Tanzania, Malawi, and Mozambique</u>.

Warren St. John, Outcasts United

ACTIVITY 3: IMITATING

Both lists of sentence parts imitate the same model sentence. Write out each imitation sentence, underline its opener, and then imitate the same model. Build your sentence in a similar way.

Write nonfiction content about one of these topics: history, biography, science, journalism, music, sports, religion, technology, art, politics, entertainment, animals, health, business, literature, psychology, or another nonfiction topic. Investigate online or offline for details about your topic.

EXAMPLE

Model to Imitate: Curiously, in summer and winter, maggots are uncommon in dumpsters.

Lars Eighner, "Dumpster Diving"

Sample Imitation One	Sample Imitation Two
a. Tragically,	**a.** Annually,
b. from 1845 to 1852	**b.** in income and other holdings
c. the Irish potato **famine** [*food scarcity*]	**c.** business **magnate** [*tycoon*] Bill Gates
d. resulted in widespread deaths.	**d.** was the wealthiest in the world.

Student's Imitation of the Same Model

Amazingly, in height and expense, the Dubai skyscraper Burj Khalifa is the world's tallest and costliest building.

Model One: Lost in his studies, Oppenheimer worked to develop the atom bomb and paid little attention to the outside world.

Steve Sheinkin, *Bomb*

Sample Imitation One	Sample Imitation Two
1a. Aware of the injustice,	**2a. Acclaimed** [*famous*] for his art,
1b. Jackie Robinson wanted to destroy all racial discrimination	**2b.** Picasso experimented to create the cubist movement
1c. and worked very hard on that important goal.	**2c.** and painted many works in his French studio.

Model Two: Because the railroads published schedules, the country was divided into four time zones.

Stephen E. Ambrose, *Nothing Like It in the World*

Sample Imitation One	Sample Imitation Two
1a. After the troops returned stateside,	**2a.** When the singers embraced Motown,
1b. the women were **relegated** [*lowered*]	**2b.** the audience was schooled
1c. to **mundane** [*trivial*] domestic chores.	**2c.** in **funky** [*jazzy*] pulsing rhythm.

Model Three: Suddenly, when we had gone ten yards, the procession to the gallows stopped short without any order or warning.

George Orwell, *A Hanging*

Sample Imitation One	Sample Imitation Two
1a. Compulsively,	**2a.** Alarmingly,
1b. after the sufferer has fasted for days,	**2b.** after a victim has been bitten by a king cobra
1c. a person with **bulimia** [*eating disorder*]	**2c.** the **venom** [*poison*] inside the person
1d. gorges nonstop on any food or drink.	**2d.** kills within a matter of ten or fifteen minutes.

Model Four: Concerned with her father, who lay dying in the bedroom, but not wanting to miss the moon landing, Phyllis was with her father when her mother called her to come and see Neil Armstrong set foot on the moon.

Frank McCourt, Teacher Man

Sample Imitation One	Sample Imitation Two
1a. Committed to his patient,	**2a.** Upset by the news,
1b. who lay waiting in the emergency room,	**2b.** which clacked across the AP wire,
1c. but unsure about the proper strategy,	**2c.** but incapable of believing the horrible truth,
1d. the surgeon was with a colleague	**2d.** CBS anchor Walter Cronkite was on the air
1e. when his patient asked him to explain	**2e.** when the news broadcast to inform
1f. and outline the procedures planned for his recovery.	**2f.** and reveal President Kennedy lay dead in Parkland Memorial Hospital.

Model Five: When Ulysses S. Grant and Robert E. Lee met in the parlor of a modest house at Appomattox Court House, Virginia, on April 9, 1865, to work out the terms for the surrender of Lee's Army of Northern Virginia, a great chapter in American life came to a close, and a great new chapter began.

Bruce Catton, The American Story

Sample Imitation One	Sample Imitation Two
1a. When James Watson and Francis Crick	**2a.** When new President Harry Truman
1b. suggested for the first time a double helix model of DNA in the journal *Nature* in 1953	**2b.** ordered during the second World War a nuclear weapon against the Japanese in August 1945
1c. to describe the building blocks of genetics in the human cell,	**2c.** to force the quick surrender of the Japanese government,
1d. an important marker in genetic research took its place,	**2d.** a dark **precedent** [*example*] in human history was introduced,
1e. and new markers began.	**2e.** and a frightening future loomed.

The beginning is the most important part of the work.

—Plato, *philosopher*

THE S-V SPLIT: GOOD MIDDLES

Sometimes, good writers use sentence tools in the middle of a sentence—between a subject and its verb—because that's the best place for the information. Take a look at sentences without tools in the middle, and then contrast them with sentences with tools in the middle called *S-V splits* because they split the subject from its verb.

An S-V split is a sentence tool between a subject and its verb with a comma before and after it.

1a. The hangman produced a small cotton bag like a flour bag and drew it down over the prisoner's face.

1b. The hangman, <u>standing still on the gallows</u>, produced a small cotton bag like a flour bag and drew it down over the prisoner's face.

George Orwell, "A Hanging"

2a. The Declaration of Independence showed that the colonies wanted to be free.

2b. The Declaration of Independence, <u>which was signed by members of the Continental Congress on July 4, 1776</u>, showed that the colonies wanted to be free.

Kay Moore, *If You Lived at the Time of the American Revolution*

3a. In New York, Democrats were joyous and Republicans angry and gloomy.

3b. In New York, <u>the most important state in any Presidential race, and a state where politics were particularly sensitive to the views of various nationality and minority groups</u>, Democrats were joyous and Republicans angry and gloomy.

John F. Kennedy, *Profiles in Courage*

ACTIVITY 1: MATCHING

Match the S-V split with its sentence. Write out each sentence, inserting the S-V split at the caret mark (^) and underlining it. **Punctuation:** Use a comma before and after each S-V split.

Sentence	S-V Split
1. The 100,000-member Jewish community of Iran, ^ , fell into **disarray** [*confusion*]. Roya Hakakian, *Journey from the Land of No*	**a.** a biggish one with a two-inch wingspread
2. The car, ^ , had a **parquet** [*wooden*] dashboard, and splintery wooden doors. Maya Angelou, *The Heart of a Woman*	**b.** the second largest community of Jews in the Middle East, after Israel
3. The end of the track, ^ , was the only spot that mattered. Stephen E. Ambrose, *Nothing Like It in the World*	**c.** not all of them of the **bohemian** [*nonconformist*] type
4. Quite a number of people, ^ , are willing to brag that they found this or that piece in the trash. Lars Eighner, "On Dumpster Diving"	**d.** the place where the rails gave out
5. A golden female moth, ^ , flapped in the fire of the candle, drooped abdomen into the wet wax, stuck, flamed, and frazzled in a second. Annie Dillard, "Death of a Moth"	**e.** a sea-green, ten-year-old Chrysler

ACTIVITY 2: COMBINING

Combine each pair of sentences by making the underlined part an S-V split to insert at the caret mark (^). Write out the result—the author's original sentence. Use a comma before and after the S-V split.

EXAMPLE

Two Sentences

The postmistress, ^ , presided over a falling-apart post office. She was a gaunt woman who wears a rawhide jacket and denims and cowboy boots.

One Sentence with S-V Split

The postmistress, a gaunt woman who wears a rawhide jacket and denims and cowboy boots, presided over a falling-apart post office.

Truman Capote, *In Cold Blood*

1. Government aid, ^ , took many forms. This kind of aid was something which began with Lincoln.
   Stephen E. Ambrose, *Nothing Like It in the World*

2. My instructor, Donald Defler, ^ , paced at the front of the lecture hall and flipped on an overhead projector. He was a **gnomish** [*dwarfish*] balding man.
   Rebecca Skloot, *The Immortal Life of Henrietta Lacks*

3. One day a group of native people, ^ , came upon the river valley. The group was <u>searching for a place to settle</u>.

Lynne Cherry, A River Ran Wild

4. A great book, ^ , demands the most active reading of which you are capable. That is the kind of book that is <u>rich in ideas and beauty, a book that raises and tries to answer great fundamental questions</u>.

Mortimer Adler, "How to Mark a Book"

5. The other woman, ^ , finished her training, married her doctor, accompanied him to Germany when he was in the service, bore three sons and a daughter, now grown and gone. She was someone <u>whose illness was diagnosed when she was eighteen</u>.

Nancy Mairs, Plaintext

ACTIVITY 3: IMITATING

Both lists of sentence parts imitate the same model sentence. Write out each imitation sentence, underline its S-V split, and then imitate the same model. Build your sentence in a similar way

Write nonfiction content about one of these topics: history, biography, science, journalism, music, sports, religion, technology, art, politics, entertainment, animals, health, business, literature, psychology, or another nonfiction topic. Investigate online or offline for details about your topic.

EXAMPLE

Model to Imitate: Sergeant Fales, a big broad-faced man, who had fought in Panama and during the Gulf War, felt anger with the pain.

Mark Bowden, Black Hawk Down

Sample Imitation One	Sample Imitation Two
a. The Hope Diamond,	**a.** The planet Mars,
b. the world's much-publicized jewel,	**b.** the second smallest Solar System planet
c. which has attracted millions at the Smithsonian Museum	**c.** which has hosted three spacecraft in orbit and two on its surface,
d. has a history of **alleged** [*unproven*] curses.	**d.** has the color of pale red.

Student's Imitation of the Same Model

Michael Phelps, the Olympic gold-medal swimmer, who holds the most gold medals of any Olympic athlete, created a foundation for promoting healthy lifestyles.

> ***Model One:*** Miss Toshiko Sasaki, the East Asia Tin Works clerk, who was not related to Dr. Sasaki, got up at three o'clock in the morning on the day the bomb fell.
>
> John Hersey, *Hiroshima*

Sample Imitation One	Sample Imitation Two
1a. *Jane Eyre,*	**2a.** Steamed hard crabs,
1b. a Victorian literary classic,	**2b.** small, red ugly **crustaceans** [*shellfish*],
1c. which has survived for generations,	**2c.** which live in the Chesapeake Bay,
1d. demonstrates strength in a woman for any era.	**2d.** bring pleasure to **famished** [*starving*] eaters at outdoor events.

Model Two: Electric bulbs, in fixtures that combined gas and electricity, were just beginning to light the newest buildings.
Erik Larson, *The Devil in the White City*

Sample Imitation One	Sample Imitation Two
1a. Hybrid power,	**2a.** The diatonic scale,
1b. in vehicles that combine gas and electricity,	**2b.** in musical shorthand that indicates notes and their durations,
1c. is now starting	**2c.** has always helped
1d. to receive greater acceptance.	**2d.** to teach **budding** [*new*] musicians.

Model Three: Pressure against the body, by a finger or the end of a pencil, causes a tarantula to move off slowly for a short distance.
Alexander Petrunkevitch, "The Spider and the Wasp"

Sample Imitation One	Sample Imitation Two
1a. Noise around a deer,	**2a.** Threats to the journalists,
1b. by a hunter or another nearby animal,	**2b.** by a famous and powerful Hollywood star,
1c. causes a deer	**2c.** caused the reporters
1d. to **flee** [*run*] quickly from the scene.	**2d.** to **refrain** [*stop*] instantly from snapping pictures.

Model Four: Vaughn Cannon, one of those tall, blond Westerners, the builders of places like Las Vegas and Los Angeles, whose eyes seem to have been bleached by the sun, was in the shop of the Young Electric Sign Company.
Tom Wolfe, *The Kandy-Kolored Tangerine-Flake Streamlined Baby*

Sample Imitation One	Sample Imitation Two
1a. Animation,	**2a.** Steve Jobs,
1b. one of the cinematic, magical techniques,	**2b.** front-runner of computer pioneers,
1c. the technique of movies like *Shrek* and *Despicable Me*,	**2c.** the creator of iEverythings like iPhones and iPads,
1d. whose **illustrations** [*drawings*] seem to **replicate** [*imitate*] actual motion,	**2d.** whose strategy was to blend function and style with usability,
1e. is really a series of motionless shots.	**2e.** was at the **helm** [*head*] of Apple, Incorporated.

Model Five: TeLinde, one of the top cervical cancer experts in the country, was a **dapper** [*stylish*] and serious fifty-six-year-old surgeon who walked with an extreme limp from an ice-skating accident.

Rebecca Skloot, *The Immortal Life of Henrietta Lacks*

Sample Imitation One	Sample Imitation Two
1a. Elvis,	**2a.** Eisenhower,
1b. one of the most **renowned** [*famous*] popular singers of the '50s and '60s,	**2b.** the 34th President of the United States,
1c. was a handsome and star-quality performer	**2c.** was a military genius and five-star general
1d. who sang with a recognizable voice in a blend of country and rock.	**2d.** who graduated from West Point with qualities of leadership.

I think we're right there in the middle of it.
I feel pretty good about it.

—Tracey Borchardt, athlete

THE CLOSER: GOOD ENDINGS

Sometimes good writers use sentence tools at the end of a sentence because that's the best place for a lasting impression. Take a look at sentences without tools at the end, and then contrast them with sentences with tools at the end called *closers* because they come at the end of the sentence.

---

*A closer is a sentence tool at the end
of the sentence preceded by a comma.*

1a. Frogs eat everything whole.

1b. Frogs eat everything whole, stuffing their **prey** [*victim*] into their mouths with their thumbs.

Annie Dillard, Pilgrim at Tinker Creek

2a. One of the last scenes for *The Perfect Storm* to be filmed was in Gloucester at St. Peter's Church.

2b. One of the last scenes for *The Perfect Storm* to be filmed was in Gloucester at St. Peter's Church, where 700 locals were hired to shoot a memorial for the dead fishermen.

Sebastian Junger, The Perfect Storm

3a. His office faced south.

3b. His office faced south, as did Root's, to satisfy their craving for natural light, a universal hunger throughout Chicago, where gas jets, still the primary source of artificial illumination, did little to **pierce** [*cut*] the city's **perpetual** [*constant*] coal-smoke dusk.

Erik Larson, The Devil in the White City

ACTIVITY 1: MATCHING

Match the closer with its sentence. Write out each sentence, inserting the closer at the caret mark (^) and underlining it. **Punctuation:** Use a comma before each closer.

Sentence	Closer
1. The spiders lie on their sides, ^ . Annie Dillard, "Death of a Moth"	**a.** his great mound of a side painfully rising and falling
2. The lovely old train station was crumbling, ^ . Tracy Kidder, *Home Town*	**b.** long since **disintegrated** [*destroyed*], whose outlines remind us how detailed, vibrant, and alive are the things of this earth that **perish** [*die*]
3. Sometimes one finds in fossil stones the **imprint** [*image*] of a leaf, ^ . Diane Ackerman, *A Natural History of the Senses*	**c.** its roof half caved in
4. The elephant was breathing very rhythmically with long rattling gasps, ^ . George Orwell, "Shooting an Elephant"	**d.** **translucent** [*semitransparent*] and ragged, their legs drying in knots
5. Tarantulas customarily live in deep cylindrical burrows, ^ . Alexander Petrunkevitch, "The Spider and the Wasp"	**e.** from which they **emerge** [*appear*] at dusk and into which they retire at dawn

ACTIVITY 2: COMBINING

Combine each pair of sentences by making the underlined part *a closer* to insert at the caret mark (^). Write out the result—the author's original sentence. Use a comma before the closer.

Two Sentences

They hung up their rifles and changed their ways, ^ . They did this with each peaceably fading into history after shaking things up, leaving their trails for others to follow.

One Sentence with Closer

They hung up their rifles and changed their ways, each peaceably fading into history after shaking things up, leaving their trails for others to follow.

Aron Ralston, *Between a Rock and a Hard Place*

---

1. The apartment was small, ^ . It was an apartment with slanting floors and irregular heat and an **inoperable** [*broken*] downstairs buzzer.

Barack Obama, *Dreams from My Father*

2. The good news is that we Americans are governed under a unique Constitution, ^ . It is a document which allows us to write whatever we please without fear of punishment.

Kurt Vonnegut, "How to Write with Style"

3. The dictionary had a picture of an aardvark, ^ . This animal is a long-tailed, long-eared, **burrowing** [*digging*] African **mammal** [*animal*] living off termites caught by sticking out its tongue as an anteater does for ants.

Malcolm X and Alex Haley, *The Autobiography of Malcolm X*

4. My father the watchmaker had a suit jacket with four huge inside pockets, ^ . The four pockets were each fitted with hooks for a dozen watches so that wherever he went the hum of hundreds of little wheels went gaily with him.

Corrie ten Boom, The Hiding Place

5. A baseball is made of a composition-cork **nucleus** [*center*], ^ . It is encased in two thin layers of rubber, one black and one red, surrounded by 12 yards of tightly wrapped blue-gray wool yarn, 45 yards of white wool yarn, 54 more yards of blue-gray wool yarn, 150 yards of fine cotton yarn, a coat of rubber cement, and a cowhide (formerly horsehide) exterior, which is held together with 216 slightly raised red cotton stitches.

Roger Angell, Five Seasons

ACTIVITY 3: IMITATING

Both lists of sentence parts imitate the same model sentence. Write out each imitation sentence, underline its closer, and then imitate the same model. Build your sentence in a similar way.

Write nonfiction content about one of these topics: history, biography, science, journalism, music, sports, religion, technology, art, politics, entertainment, animals, health, business, literature, psychology, or another interesting topic. Investigate online or offline for details about your topic.

- -

EXAMPLE

Model to Imitate: Belmont's racing course was War Admiral's home track, the **site** [*place*] of that horse's greatest performance.

Laura Hillenbrand, Seabiscuit

Sample Imitation One	Sample Imitation Two
1a. Elvis Presley's brother	**2a.** Salk's polio vaccine
1b. was Jessie Presley,	**2b.** was a medical miracle,
1c. the stillborn identical twin of that famous singer.	**2c.** the reason for that scientist's lasting **legacy** [*reputation*].

Student's Imitation of the Same Model

Gettysburg was the site of a major Civil War battle, a field in Pennsylvania that saw over 8,000 men and 3,000 horses killed.

Model One: Children love to play in piles of leaves, **hurling** [*throwing*] them into the air like confetti, leaping into soft **unruly** [*disorderly*] mattresses of them.

Diane Ackerman, *A Natural History of the Senses*

Sample Imitation One	Sample Imitation Two
1a. Dogs like to sniff in cans of garbage,	**2a.** Bees like to nest near lots of flowers,
1b. pulling goodies out from the can like treats,	**2b.** eating **nectar** [*sweet liquid*] from the blooms like snacks,
1c. searching for tasty food scraps within the **refuse** [*trash*].	**2c.** burrowing into fragrant appetizing masses of them.

Model Two: The oldest two Fahey boys were there, polite blond boys who lived near me on Lloyd Street, and who had four brothers and sisters.

Annie Dillard, *An American Childhood*

Sample Imitation One	Sample Imitation Two
1a. The fat furry slinking mongoose	**2a.** The renowned women gymnasts
1b. was there,	**2b.** were there,
1c. a **predator** [*killing*] animal	**2c.** petite **agile** [*flexible*] women
1d. who kills poisonous snakes in fights	**2d.** who competed against others on all events
1e. and who is resistant or immune to snake **venom** [*poison*].	**2e.** and who were cheered and applauded by **avid** [*intense*] fans.

Model Three: The space around the solar system is populated by huge numbers of comets, small worlds a few miles in diameter, rich in water and the other chemicals **essential** [*necessary*] to life.

Kenneth Brower, *The Starship and the Canoe*

Sample Imitation One	Sample Imitation Two
1a. The tanks inside an aquarium	**2a.** The area near the Atlantic Ocean
1b. are alive with different breeds of fish,	**2b.** is characterized by small sections of marsh,
1c. unusual fish an assortment of species,	**2c.** interesting **habitats** [*communities*] a range of sizes and shapes
1d. varied in color	**2d.** home to **ecosystems** [*habitats*]
1e. and other characteristics needed for classification.	**2e.** and the temporary stopovers for **migratory** [*traveling*] birds.

Model Four: Because he is so old, and has survived so many difficult journeys, he has become the most celebrated shorebird in the world.

Phillip Hoose, *Moonbird*

Sample Imitation One	Sample Imitation Two
1a. Because it is so large,	**2a.** Because it is so terrifying,
1b. and has **astounded** [*amazed*] so many museum visitors,	**2b.** and has **populated** [*inhabited*] so many horror films,
1c. the Hope Diamond	**2c.** the Tyrannosaurus Rex
1d. has become the most **acclaimed** [*famous*] jewel in modern history.	**2d.** has become the most recognizable dinosaur in the movies.

Model Five: One of the few scientific **treatises** [*papers*] ever written on the subject of bravery is *The Anatomy of Courage* by Charles Moran, who served as a doctor in the trenches for the British in World War I, and who was better known later as Lord Moran, personal physician to Winston Churchill.

Tom Wolfe, *The Right Stuff*

Sample Imitation One	Sample Imitation Two
1a. One of the best young quarterbacks ever signed to the National League was Johnny Unitas,	**2a.** An example of a devastating political strategy during the era of the Cold War was the Berlin Wall,
1b. who served as a **linchpin** [*anchor*] for the Baltimore Colts in the early years of that league,	**2b.** which acted as a **barricade** [*block*] between the east and west in the city of Berlin after World War II,
1c. and who was in 1979 inducted into the Hall of Fame,	**2c.** and which became an **iconic** [*famous*] symbol of oppression,
1d. a recognition of his golden arm.	**2d.** a block to coexistence.

- -

The practice of analyzing and imitating sentences
is also the practice of learning how to read
them with an informed appreciation.

Stanley Fish, *How to Write a Sentence: And How to Read One*

- -

THE MIX: SENTENCE SALADS

In the previous sections, you learned and practiced sentence-composing tools as *openers*, *S-V splits*, and *closers*. In this section, you'll practice using a mix of those positions.

A mix is two or three of the tool positions—opener, S-V split, closer—within the same sentence.

On a Sunday evening in Chicago, October 8, 1871, a fire started that, over the next three days, resulted in destruction and death in an area three and one-third miles in size: property damage and destruction of 192,000 million dollars; deaths of 300 people; and homelessness for over 100,000. The fire started in the barn owned by Mr. and Mrs. Patrick and Catherine O'Leary, and gave rise to the popular verse:

One dark night, when people were in bed,

Mrs. O'Leary lit a lantern in her shed,

The cow kicked it over, winked its eye, and said,

There'll be a hot time in the old town tonight.

Although catchy and memorable, that humorous poem is probably untrue. In his thoroughly researched account of the origin of that fire, author Jim Murphy's version in *The Great Fire* is more believable.

Notice how much more information is in the original paragraph, conveyed through sentence tools in a mix of positions: *opener*, *S-V split*, *closer*.

WITHOUT TOOLS: (115 words)

(1) Sullivan crossed the street, and sat down on the wooden sidewalk. (2) He leaned back against the fence to enjoy the night.

(3) The wind had been strong all day. (4) He first saw the fire. (5) Sullivan made his way directly to the barn to save the animals inside. (6) The barn's loft held over three tons of hay. (7) Flames from the burning hay pushed against the roof and beams. (8) A shower of burning embers greeted Sullivan. (9) The heat was fiercely intense and blinding. (10) Sullivan slipped on the uneven floorboards. (11) Sullivan discovered that his wooden leg had gotten stuck between two boards and come off.

TOOLS IN MIXED POSITIONS (Bolded):
(180 words, with one-third tools)

(1) Sullivan, **ambling down a stretch of land**, crossed the street, and sat down on the wooden sidewalk. (2) **Adjusting his wooden leg to make himself comfortable**, he leaned back against the fence to enjoy the night. (3) The wind, **coming off the prairie**, had been strong all day, **gusting wildly sometimes, with leaves scuttling across the street**. (4) **While he pushed himself up to go home**, he first saw the fire, **a single tongue of flame, shooting out the side of O'Leary's barn**. (5) Sullivan made his way directly to the barn to save the animals inside. (6) The barn's loft held over three tons of hay, **delivered earlier that day**. (7) Flames from the burning hay pushed against the roof and beams, **as if they were struggling to break free**. (8) **As he entered the building**, a shower of burning embers greeted Sullivan. (9) The heat was fiercely intense and blinding. (10) **In his rush to flee**, Sullivan slipped on the uneven floorboards, **falling with a thud**. (11) **As he struggled to get up**, Sullivan discovered that his wooden leg had gotten stuck between two boards and come off.

Jim Murphy, *The Great Fire*

TOOLS BY POSITION

Important: Notice that each tool is a *sentence part*, not a complete sentence.

OPENERS (*tools at the beginning of a sentence*)

- adjusting his wooden leg to make himself comfortable
- while he pushed himself up to go home
- as he entered the building
- in his rush to flee
- as he struggled to get up

S-V SPLITS (*tools between a subject and verb*)

- **ambling** down a stretch of land
- coming off the prairie

CLOSERS (*tools at the end of a sentence*)

- gusting wildly sometimes
- with leaves **scuttling** across the street
- delivered earlier that day
- as if they were struggling to break free
- falling with a thud

Clearly, the paragraph with mixed tools is much stronger than the paragraph without tools, providing more information, important details, and mature style. Using sentence-composing tools within your own sentences—*openers, S-V splits, closers,* and *mixes*—strengthens your writing.

ACTIVITY 1: MATCHING

These sentences mix tool positions—openers, S-V splits, closers. Add sentence tools at the caret marks (^). Write out and punctuate the sentence, underline each tool, and name its position (*opener, S-V split, closer*).

Sentences	Tools
1. ^ , he'd built the house on his own, ^ . Rebecca Skloot, *The Immortal Life of Henrietta Lacks*	**a.** on a Saturday afternoon in July 1938 / appearing confused and disoriented
2. ^ , Tommy was talking to a former gang member named Felix, ^ . Tracy Kidder, *Home Town*	**b.** though Cootie could barely move his arms / teaching himself construction as he went along, hammering the plywood walls, and plastering the inside
3. ^ , a half-starved teenager wandered into a bus station in Columbus, Ohio, ^ . Laura Hillenbrand, *Seabiscuit*	**c.** once, at the Library of Congress in Washington / a Confederate bank note, perhaps **acquired** [*gotten*] during the president's recent **excursion** [*trip*] to the fallen capital of Richmond, and a pocket knife
4. ^ , I was shown the contents of Lincoln's pockets on the night that he was shot at Ford's Theater, ^ . Gore Vidal, "Lincoln Up Close"	**d.** about a year after the incident / a young man he'd known as a baby
5. ^ , we held our working cards from the shop, ^ . Gerda Weissmann Klein, "All But My Life"	**e.** in our clenched fists / those sacred cards that we thought meant security

ACTIVITY 2: ARRANGING

Below are shortened sentences. The sentence tools from the original sentences are randomly listed underneath.

1. Insert the tools in at least two different positions—*opener*, *S-V split*, *closer*.

2. Write the sentence, adding commas where needed.

3. Name the tool positions (*opener*, *S-V split*, *closer*).

4. Finally, using your arranged sentence as a model, write an imitation.

EXAMPLE

Shortened Sentence: Bob spoke only in monosyllables.

TOOLS TO ARRANGE

a. avoiding eye contact

b. pale and drawn

c. his brown hair **unkempt** [*messy*]

Result (other arrangements are acceptable): His brown hair unkempt, pale and drawn, Bob spoke only in monosyllables, avoiding eye contact. (*opener*, *closer*)

Imitation: Tan and handsome, his hand extended, President Kennedy moved congenially among the crowd, greeting his admirers.

Original Sentence: Pale and drawn, his brown hair unkempt, Bob spoke only in monosyllables, avoiding eye contact.
Dina Ingber, "Computer Addicts"

---

1. He was up on the roof of the family house when he slipped and fell.

   a. breaking his left arm below the elbow

   b. when my father was fourteen

   Roald Dahl, *Boy*

2. I went out of the library.

   a. fearing that the librarian would call me back for further questioning

   b. not daring to glance at the books

   Richard Wright, *Black Boy*

3. I took my son.

   a. who had never had any fresh water up his nose

   b. on the fishing trip

   c. and who had seen lily pads only from train windows

   E. B. White, "Once More to the Lake"

4. I found my pet's skinned body.

   a. with the braces still on his crippled front legs,

   b. lying on the dump

   c. a few days later

   Wallace Stegner, *A History, a Story,*
   and a Memory of the Last Plains Frontier

5. Anne was living with her father and mother and her sister Margot.

    a. in a housing development in Amsterdam

    b. who was three years older than Anne

    c. during the war in 1942

    Ruud Van Der Roi, *Anne Frank*

6. Claudette Colvin boarded the Highland Gardens bus with a few of her friends and slid into a window seat on the left side.

    a. a slim, bespectacled high school junior

    b. behind the white section of the bus

    c. around 3:30 on March 2, 1955

    Phillip Hoose, *Claudette Colvin: Twice Toward Justice*

7. The electric current **distorts** [*changes*] normal **ventricular** [*heart*] rhythm into an ineffective wormlike wriggling called fibrillation.

    a. which has the same effect as cardiac arrest

    b. by passing through the heart

    c. during the death penalty

    Sherman B. Nuland, "Cruel and Unusual"

8. Technicians were able to gradually reduce the size of the gas bubble.

    a. using a special apparatus from the atomic laboratory at Oak Ridge, Tennessee

    b. the danger of a catastrophic release of radioactive materials over

    c. working desperately

    Barry Commoner, *The Politics of Energy*

9. The story of *Ender's Game* is the one that readers create in their minds.

    a. guided and shaped by my text

    b. but then **transformed** [*changed*], expanded, edited, and clarified by their own experience, their own desires, their own hopes and fears

    c. the true story

    > Orson Scott Card, "Introduction" to *Ender's Game*

10. A young man spotted me.

    a. obviously fresh from a pub

    b. and went down on his knees in the aisle

    c. breaking into his Irish tenor's rendition of "Maria" from *West Side Story*

    d. on a bus trip to London from Oxford University

    > Judith Ortiz Cofer, "The Myth of the Latin Woman"

YOUR TURN: PERSONALITY PROFILE

Use sentence-composing tools effectively by writing several paragraphs profiling a special person in your life—as in the example below titled "My Prestidigitator." A prestidigitator is a magician. Jenny Crocker, the author, thought of her grandfather as someone who worked magic in her young life.

Like Jenny's profile of her grandfather, include in order four glimpses of the person you profile:

- a statement of the lasting impression the person made on you

- a physical description of the person

- a setting where the person is present

- and a significant event involving the person.

End your profile with a short sentence emphasizing the impact the person had on your life. The sample profile "My Prestidigitator" ends with Jenny's comment: "I adored him."

IMPORTANCE OF THE SENTENCE-COMPOSING TOOLS

Contrast the two versions of the personality profile by Jenny below—the first mostly without *openers*, *S-V splits*, *closers*, *mixes*; the second with an abundance of those tools. In the personality profile you write, aim for lots of sentence-composing tools like the second version, which is a sample of a good personality profile.

"My Prestidigitator"

(1) From some people we get insight, understanding, friendship, knowledge. (2) From my grandfather I got all these and more. (3) He made magic in my life.

(4) Granddaddy was not someone who smothered my two sisters and me with kisses or scooped us up into his arms or onto his lap. (5) He was bald. (6) He always wore a suit, a freshly starched shirt, and a bowtie, and it was impossible for me to imagine him in, well, pajamas. (7) He always placed peppermints for us to find. (8) We would come up with a fistful of candy. (9) I couldn't wait to see him.

(10) Our family would go from our house in the country to his house in the city for dinner. (11) He lived in a large brick house. (12) We traveled almost an hour from the farm on which we were raised. (13) Granddaddy's house was another world: instead of the country fields we were used to, there was a manicured back yard; instead of a barn, a garage with an automatic door; instead of comfortably muddied scatter rugs, well-kept Orientals; instead of

spilled milk from the latest litter of kittens, a spotless and shining kitchen floor.

(14) Our parents dubbed these visits "the culture course." (15) Mama sought to provide at least a veneer of civility over her hopelessly countrified granddaughters. (16) We convened at a formal dining room table.

(17) A gaffe in gentility at this table was acknowledged by our grandmother with a reprimand, an embarrassment our parents tried to prevent by drilling us in manners during the long car ride from the country to the city. (18) Such efforts were largely unsuccessful. (19) My sisters and I understood, however, that my parents could not intervene on our behalf if we made a mistake.

(20) "Jenny, unfold your napkin before you put it in your lap."

(21) "Yes ma'am."

(22) "Don't play with it now that it's in your lap."

(23) "Yes, ma'am."

(24) That was pretty much the extent of our conversations.

(25) Granddaddy was our only hope of rescue or relief. (26) Once when Mama asked him to pass the biscuits, he picked one out of the basket and tossed it to her. (27) "Oh, Francis!" she said disapprovingly, but her tinkling laughter reverberated like the sound of clinking teacups. (28) Granddaddy was on the side of the children.

(29) I adored him.

A house isn't complete after its foundation is built: it needs additions—walls, windows, floors, roof, and so forth. A sentence isn't complete with just a foundation—a subject and a predicate. It needs additions—*openers, S-V splits, closers, mixes.*

The first version of "My Prestidigitator" consists of just foundation sentences—basic sentences without *openers, S-V splits, closers,* or *mixes.* The second and stronger version builds lots of elaboration onto sentence foundations by adding *openers, S-V splits, closers,* and *mixes.*

Now study the version below with tools. Notice the power those varied tools—*openers*, *S-V splits*, *closers*—provide.

Sample Personality Profile of a Memorable Person

(Sentence-composing tools are underlined.)

"My Prestidigitator"

by Jenny Crocker

(1) From some people, we get insight; from some, understanding; from others, friendship; from still others, knowledge. (2) From my grandfather, I got all these and more. (3) He made magic in my life.

(4) Granddaddy, a reserved gentleman, was not someone who smothered my two sisters and me with kisses or scooped us up into his arms or onto his lap. (5) Tall and thin and **austere** [*stern*] until he smiled, he was bald, except for a neatly trimmed fringe, which ran around his head from ear to ear like a railroad track. (6) He always wore a suit, a freshly starched shirt, and a bowtie, and it was impossible for me to imagine him in, well, pajamas. (7) In the pockets of his suit coat, he always placed peppermints for us to find. (8) Running to him and reaching up into those pockets, we would come up with a fistful of candy. (9) Though he had only hard angles where soft places might have been, no pot belly or snuggle-spots in his spare frame, I couldn't wait to see him.

(10) On most Sundays and on an occasional week-night, our family, which consisted of Mom and Dad and sisters Toni and Dotty, would go from our house in the country to his house in the city for dinner. (11) He lived in a large brick house, on a quietly **affluent** [*wealthy*], tree-lined street in the city. (12) We traveled almost an hour from the farm on which we were raised. (13) For us, Granddaddy's house was another world: instead of the country fields we were used to, there was a manicured back yard; instead of a barn, a garage with an automatic

door; instead of comfortably muddied scatter rugs, well-kept Orientals; instead of spilled milk from the latest litter of kittens, a spotless and shining kitchen floor.

(14) To soften our grandmother's obvious disappointment in how we were turning out, our parents **dubbed** [*named*] these visits "the culture course." (15) Mama, our maternal grandmother, among the last of the Victorian ladies, sought to provide at least a **veneer** [*layer*] of civility over her hopelessly countrified granddaughters. (16) Changed from the denim and dirt of the farm, attired **immaculately** [*perfectly*] in freshly laundered dresses and black patent leather shoes, we **convened** [*gathered*] at a formal dining room table, furnished with all the trappings of the well-to-do: china, crystal, linen tablecloth and napkins, **doilies** [*lace*] underneath the glasses of tomato juice served on their own **translucent** [*semitransparent*] china plates, a silver bell to beckon a servant from the kitchen, a sweet, **taciturn** [*quiet*] lady named, ironically, "Belle."

(17) A **gaffe** [*mistake*] in **gentility** [*manners*] at this table was acknowledged by our grandmother with a **reprimand** [*scolding*], an embarrassment our parents tried to prevent by drilling us in manners during the long car ride from the country to the city. (18) Such efforts were largely unsuccessful. (19) My sisters and I understood, however, that my parents could not **intervene** [*argue*] on our behalf if we made a mistake, because at this table our grandmother **reigned** [*ruled*] supreme.

(20) "Jenny, unfold your napkin before you put it in your lap."

(21) "Yes, ma'am."

(22) "Don't play with it now that it's in your lap."

(23) "Yes, ma'am."

(24) That was pretty much the extent of our conversations.

(25) Granddaddy, a reluctant partner in our culture course, was our only hope of rescue or relief. (26) Once when Mama asked him to pass the biscuits, he picked one out of the basket and tossed it to her. (27) "Oh, Francis!" she said disapprovingly, but her tinkling

laughter **reverberated** [*sounded*] like the sound of clinking teacups.
(28) Granddaddy, I always felt, was on the side of the children.
   (29) I adored him.

Throughout your profile, use sentence-composing tools of different types, lengths, and positions (*openers*, *S-V splits*, *closers*, *mixes*). Below are varied examples for each position from Jenny's profile of her grandfather.

OPENERS

- In the pockets of his suit coat, he always placed peppermints for us to find.

- Though he had only hard angles where soft places might have been, no pot belly or snuggle-spots in his spare frame, I couldn't wait to see him. (*Contains two openers.*)

- To soften our grandmother's obvious disappointment in how we were turning out, our parents dubbed these visits "the culture course."

- Once, when Mama asked him to pass the biscuits, he picked one out of the basket and tossed it to her. (*Contains two openers.*)

S-V SPLITS

- Granddaddy, a reserved gentleman, was not someone who smothered my two sisters and me with kisses or scooped us up into his arms or onto his lap.

- Mama, our maternal grandmother, among the last of the Victorian ladies, sought to provide at least a veneer of civility over her hopelessly countrified granddaughters. (*Contains two openers.*)

- Granddaddy, <u>a reluctant partner in the culture course</u>, was our only hope of rescue or relief.

CLOSERS

- He lived in a large brick house, <u>on a quietly affluent, tree-lined street in Baltimore city.</u>

- A gaffe in gentility at this table was acknowledged by our grandmother with a reprimand, <u>an embarrassment our parents tried to prevent by drilling us in etiquette during the long car ride from the country to the city.</u>

- My sisters and I understood, however, that my parents could not intervene on our behalf if we made a mistake, <u>because at this table our grandmother reigned supreme.</u>

MIXES

- <u>Tall and thin and austere-looking until he smiled</u>, he was bald, <u>except for a neatly trimmed fringe</u>, which ran around his head from ear to ear <u>like a railroad track.</u> (*opener* and *closer*)

- <u>On most Sundays and on an occasional week-night</u>, our family, <u>which consisted of Mom and Dad and sisters Toni and Dotty</u>, would go from our house in the country to his house in the city for dinner. (*opener* and *S-V split*)

- <u>Changed from the denim and dirt of the farm, attired immaculately in freshly laundered dresses and black patent leather shoes</u>, we convened at a formal dining room table, <u>furnished with all the trappings of the well-to-do: china, crystal, linen tablecloth and</u>

napkins, doilies underneath the glasses of tomato juice served on their own translucent china plates, a silver bell to beckon a servant from the kitchen, a sweet, taciturn lady named, ironically, "Belle." (*opener* and *closer*)

It is a matter of practice, of becoming so familiar with the tools in advance of any particular use of them that when an occasion of use turns up, you and they will be ready.

—Stanley Fish, *How to Write a Sentence: And How to Read One*

OUT OF BOUNDS: PROBLEM SENTENCES

Sentences need boundaries—places that mark the beginning and ending of a sentence—so readers can understand what they read. Spoken sentences use the sound of the voice to tell listeners where one sentence ends and the next sentence begins. Written sentences use mainly capital letters and periods for sentence boundaries: capitals at the beginning of the sentence, and periods at the end.

ACTIVITY 1: SENTENCE BOUNDARY EXERCISE

Read the two versions of the same passage below to understand the importance of boundary markers—capital letters and periods. It will be easy to tell which version lacks those markers, and which has them.

VERSION ONE

I had already found a lot of ticks crawling up my legs and had learned to pluck them off and squash them in my fingers they were red and active, and itched like mad when they dug into the skin they left an itchy little bump and, if you scratched it, you soon developed a sore there were also chiggers these **burrowed** [*dug*] under your toe-nails, laid their eggs, and created a swollen, red, tormenting place on your toe to **extract** [*remove*] it, you had to wait until the chigger was ripe Juma, our cook, was an expert at this he would seize a needle which you first held in a match-flame, grip your toe with thumb and forefinger, and plunge the needle in with such skill and **dispatch** [*speed*] that in a few moments he had cleared a pathway to the chigger and extracted on the end of his weapon the neatest little white bag, about as large as an onion seed, containing the eggs it was the female who caused all the trouble male chiggers either leapt about at large, or displayed the masculine habit of **clustering** [*gathering*] together, in this case round the eyes or ears of dogs and chickens, evidently the clubs, lodges, and messes of the chigger world I soon learned never to go barefoot, or, if I had mislaid my slippers, to walk with my toes curled up off the ground, a habit that **persisted** [*continued*] for years after chiggers had passed out of my life.

VERSION TWO

I had already found a lot of ticks crawling up my legs and had learned to pluck them off and squash them in my fingers. They were red and active, and itched like mad when they dug into the skin. They left an itchy little bump and, if you scratched it, you soon developed a sore. There were also chiggers. These burrowed under your toe-nails, laid their eggs, and created a swollen, red, tormenting place on your toe. To extract it, you had to wait until the chigger was ripe. Juma, our cook, was an expert at this. He would seize a needle which you first held in a match-flame, grip your toe with thumb and forefinger, and plunge the needle in with such skill and dispatch that in a few moments he had cleared a pathway to the chigger and extracted on the end of his weapon the neatest little white bag, about as large as an onion seed, containing the eggs. It was the female who caused all the trouble. Male chiggers either leapt about at large, or displayed the masculine habit of clustering together, in this case round the eyes or ears of dogs and chickens, evidently the clubs, lodges, and messes of the chigger world. I soon learned never to go barefoot, or, if I had mislaid my slippers, to walk with my toes curled up off the ground, a habit that persisted for years after chiggers had passed out of my life.

Elspeth Huxley, *The Flame Trees of Thika:*
Memories of an African Childhood

When sentences are "out of bounds," they go too far, or don't go far enough. In other words, they don't stick to their boundaries. With sentences, there can be three kinds of boundary problems: run-ons, comma splices, and fragments.

TOO LITTLE SENTENCE: FRAGMENTS

A fragment is "too little" sentence—a sentence part mistakenly written like a complete sentence—capital letter at the beginning, period at the end. Because readers expect a whole sentence when they see something that begins with a capital letter and ends with a period, fragments confuse readers: a fragment is just a piece of a sentence. Readers expect a whole sentence.

ACTIVITY 2: FINDING FRAGMENTS

In each list, identify four fragments and one sentence. The fragments masquerade as sentences—starting with a capital letter and ending with a period—but are actually just parts of a sentence. A sentence requires a subject and a predicate. If one or both is missing, it's a fragment—just a part of a sentence.

LIST ONE

1. Was undergoing spinal surgery in the same hospital two floors above me.

2. To demonstrate sisterhood and brotherhood with the plants and animals.

3. Which proudly advertised hot and cold running water.

4. In a long braided rope across the top of her head.

5. The study of electricity got a big boost in 1745 with the invention of the Leyden jar, the first device capable of storing and **amplifying** [*enlarging*] static electricity.

6. Walking awkwardly, my wet clothes **hindering** [*slowing*] movement.

7. The true nature of the damage to the *Titanic* may be partly revealed as exploration of the wreck continues over the coming years.

8. Small worlds a few miles in diameter, rich in water and the other chemicals essential to life.

9. Who walked with an extreme limp from an ice-skating accident more than a decade earlier.

10. Wrote without reserve about her likes and dislikes.

Only two (#5, #7) are sentences because only they contain a topic (subject) and a comment about the topic (predicate)—the two requirements for every sentence. The rest are fragments because they are sentence parts, not whole sentences. Because they start with a capital letter and end with a period, they start and end like sentences, but aren't.

Here are the original sentences. The fragments are now where they belong, parts of a whole sentence.

1. A few days after I went into the hospital for that crick in my neck, another brother, an outstanding football player in college, was undergoing spinal surgery in the same hospital two floors above me.

John McMurty, "Kill 'Em! Crush 'Em! Eat 'Em Raw!"

2. To demonstrate sisterhood and brotherhood with the plants and animals, the old-time people made masks and costumes that transformed the human figures of the dancers into the animal beings they portrayed.

Leslie Marmon Silko, *Yellow Woman and a Beauty of the Spirit*

3. I checked into the Paradise Hotel, which proudly advertised hot and cold running water.

Michael Crichton, *Travels*

4. She wore her coarse, straight hair, which was slightly streaked with gray, in a long braided rope across the top of her head.

Maya Angelou, Wouldn't Take Nothing for My Journey Now

5. **[THE ONLY SENTENCE FROM LIST ONE.]** The study of electricity got a big boost in 1745 with the invention of the Leyden jar, the first device capable of storing and amplifying static electricity.

Eric Larson, Thunderstruck

6. I followed, walking awkwardly, my wet clothes hindering movement.

Jane Goodall, Through a Window

7. **[THE ONLY SENTENCE FROM LIST TWO.]** The true nature of the damage to the *Titanic* may be partly revealed as exploration of the wreck continues over the coming years.

Walter Lord, The Night Lives On

8. The space around the solar system is populated by huge numbers of comets, small worlds a few miles in diameter, rich in water and the other chemicals essential to life.

Kenneth Brower, The Starship and the Canoe

9. The doctor, brilliant, one of the top cervical cancer experts in the country, was a dapper and serious fifty-six-year-old surgeon, who walked with an extreme limp from an ice-skating accident more than a decade earlier.

Rebecca Skloot, The Immortal Life of Henrietta Lacks

10. Anne Frank, who was thirteen when she began her diary and fifteen when she was forced to stop, wrote without reserve about her likes and dislikes.

Otto H. Frank and Mirjam Pressler (editors),
The Diary of Anne Frank

ACTIVITY 3: CONNECTING FRAGMENTS TO SENTENCES

The list on the right contains fragments to insert at the caret (^) in the appropriate sentence on the left, where they then become parts of that sentence.

Sentences	Fragments
1. ^ , he **scoffed** [*laughed*] at the idea, labeling the trucks a mere **fad** [*trend*] that would never last. Walter Dean Myers, *Bad Boy*	**a.** the result of my collision with Bryan Smith's windshield
2. In hunting season, all kinds of small **game** [*animals*] turn up in dumpsters, ^ . Lars Eighner, "On Dumpster Diving"	**b.** if a sick person folds one thousand paper cranes
3. There's a long **gash** [*cut*] in my scalp, ^ . Stephen King, *On Writing*	**c.** when trucks began to replace horses and wagons

4. ^ , the gods will grant her wish and make her healthy again.
        Eleanor Coerr,
    Sadako and the Thousand Paper Cranes
	d. where I spend a lot of my time, poaching eggs, poking a fork into the pot roast

5. The **sampler** [*picture*] I like best hangs over the stove, ^ .
        Anna Quindlen,
    Lots of Candles, Plenty of Cake
	e. some of it, sadly, not entirely dead

ACTIVITY 4: DETECTING FRAGMENTS

First, read through the paragraph to get an idea of the content. Because it has fragments, reading might be bumpy. Then, write out the paragraph while connecting each fragment to the sentence where it belongs. Afterward, reading will be smooth.

> (1) Coyotes, considered to be members of the **canine** [*dog*] family. (2) Often mate for life. (3) In recent years western coyotes have **interbred** [*mated*] with wolves. (4) Creating a new **hybrid** [*combination*], bigger and stronger. (5) One helpful **characteristic** [*aspect*] of the wolf that has now become a characteristic of the interbred coyote is a stronger and bigger jaw. (6) This jaw allows the coyote to go after different **prey** [*food*]. (7) Not just rabbits and mice. (8) The coyote is now able to take down a small deer. (9) And live off that meat for up to six or seven days. (10) These hybrid coyotes have learned how to cross bridges. (11) Because of that, they have **saturated** [*filled*] the eastern landscape. (12) Except for Long Island, New York. (13) This latest step in the **evolution** [*development*] of the coyote renders the title "top dog" with great accuracy.

ACTIVITY 5: SOLVING A FRAGMENT JIGSAW PUZZLE

This paragraph, about how the Egyptian pharaoh King Tut died, has to be put back together. Underneath the paragraph is a list of fragments that are sentence parts of the original paragraph. Fragments are listed in the order they appear in the paragraph. Connect each fragment to the sentence where it belongs. *On the Mark:* At many connections, commas are needed.

KING TUT'S MYSTERIOUS DEATH

> (1) There is one outstanding and **intriguing** [*interesting*] mystery that remains. (2) No one is actually sure. (3) The theories include that he was murdered by enemies, that he died of an infection, and that he was crushed by a hippopotamus. (4) The newest theory suggests that he

was run over by a chariot. (5) The forensic lab has examined all of the evidence put together for the first time to create a virtual autopsy. (6) The heart was also missing. (7) The scientists used a chariot made as a prop for the movies. (8) Experts decided that the most likely object is a chariot wheel. (9) They collected data on how the vehicle **maneuvered** [*reached*] its top speed. (10) The first **simulation** [*reenactment*] showed King Tut falling off his chariot, and the second showed him crashing the chariot, but neither one of these simulations matched the injuries. (11) The final **scenario** [*recreation*] showed King Tut crouched on his knees as he was dropped by the wheel of an oncoming chariot. (12) No one is ready to close the case.

FRAGMENTS

a. although much has been learned about the ancient pharaoh of Egypt called King Tutankhamen

b. in spite of many theories that suggest how the pharaoh died

c. backed up by forensic X-rays and explanations

d. which uses special equipment to solve crimes

e. revealing that King Tut's body on his left side is missing eight ribs

f. plus part of his pelvis

g. to simulate the accident as it might have happened

h. after talking about what types of objects could cause this kind of damage

i. passing their findings on to specialists who create different computer simulations

j. although the injuries line up in that simulation

TOO MUCH SENTENCE: COMMA SPLICES AND RUN-ONS

A *comma splice* is "too much" sentence—two sentences written incorrectly as one sentence—with just a comma "splicing" them together.

A *run-on* is also "too much" sentence—two sentences incorrectly written as one sentence, but with nothing between the two sentences to tell readers where one sentence ends and the next sentence begins.

Readers expect a clear boundary between two sentences, telling where one sentence ends and the next sentence begins. Comma splices and run-ons lack that boundary and cause reading problems. If you get confused reading the following example, it's not your fault. It's the fault of the comma splice.

EXAMPLE OF A COMMA SPLICE

(Based upon *The Great Fire* by Jim Murphy)

Flames from the burning hay pushed against the roof and beams as if they were struggling to break free, a shower of burning embers greeted Sullivan as he entered the building. (*two sentences with just a comma between them*)

Likewise, you'll get even more confused reading the following example—a run-on.

EXAMPLE OF A RUN-ON

Flames from the burning hay pushed against the roof and beams as if they were struggling to break free a shower of burning embers greeted Sullivan as he entered the building. (*two sentences with nothing between them*)

Note: Sentence length has nothing to do with whether something is a run-on. If two sentences have no punctuation or words between them, it's a run-on, regardless of the length of the sentence. As you will see below, something very short can be a run-on sentence, and something very long can be a correct sentence—not a run-on.

A RUN-ON: The rain stopped the game continued. (*It's a run-on between stopped and the game—where the first sentence should end, and the second one begin.*)

NOT A RUN-ON: The angry man chased Mikey and me around the yellow house and up a backyard path, under a low tree, up a bank, through a hedge, down some snowy steps, and across the grocery store's delivery driveway. (*Even though very long, it is not a run-on sentence. It is one sentence.*)

Annie Dillard, An American Childhood

Remember this: A run-on sentence results from unclear sentence boundaries, not sentence length. In this worktext you'll see many very long sentences by authors. None is a run-on.

ELIMINATING COMMA SPLICES OR RUN-ONS

There are three ways to get rid of either a comma splice or a run-on. (Examples are based upon *Enrique's Journey* by Sonia Nazario.)

(1) MAKE TWO SENTENCES: *Use a period to end the first sentence, and a capital letter to start the next sentence.*

Comma Splice: Virtually unnoticed, he will become one of an estimated 48,000 children who enter the United States from Central America and Mexico each year, illegally and without either of their parents, roughly two thirds of them will make it past the U.S. Immigration and Naturalization Service.

Run-On: Virtually unnoticed, he will become one of an estimated 48,000 children who enter the United States from Central America and Mexico each year, illegally and without either of their parents roughly two thirds of them will make it past the U.S. Immigration and Naturalization Service.

CORRECT:

Virtually unnoticed, he will become one of an estimated 48,000 children who enter the United States from Central America and Mexico each year, illegally and without either of their **parents. Roughly** two thirds of them will make it past the U.S. Immigration and Naturalization Service.

(2) ADD A COMMA PLUS *and, but, or, so, for,* or *yet* TO JOIN THE SENTENCES.

CORRECT: Virtually unnoticed, he will become one of an estimated 48,000 children who enter the United States from Central America and Mexico each year, illegally and without either of their **parents, yet roughly** two thirds of them will make it past the U.S. Immigration and Naturalization Service.

(3) USE A SEMICOLON BETWEEN THE SENTENCES. *A semicolon can replace a period if the two sentences are closely linked in meaning.*

CORRECT: Virtually unnoticed, he will become one of an estimated 48,000 children who enter the United States from Central America and Mexico each year, illegally and without either of their **parents; roughly** two thirds of them will make it past the U.S. Immigration and Naturalization Service.

ACTIVITY 6: CORRECTING COMMA SPLICES AND RUN-ONS

Numbers 1–5 contain either a comma splice or a run-on. Revise each three times, each time using a different way: first, as two separate sentences ending with periods; next, as two sentences joined by *and, but, or, so, for,* or *yet*; and finally, as two sentences joined by a semicolon.

1. Despite the widespread belief that he was the man who first discovered America, Columbus was not the first explorer to reach the Americas, he was preceded in the 11th century by Norse explorer Leif Ericson 500 years earlier, who landed on the northern tip of what is now Newfoundland in North America

2. The Boeing factory, located in Everett, Washington, is the largest building by volume in the world, with 472,370,319 cubic feet and covering 98.3 acres an airport assembly building it offers tours and includes several cafes.

3. Basically street entertainers, snake charmers take precautions to prevent the snake, usually a cobra, from harming them, mainly by sitting out of biting range also they sometimes remove the snake's venomous fangs, or even sew the snake's mouth shut.

4. In a rainbow, raindrops act like prisms, in which light enters as white light but exits as the seven colors of the spectrum, forming an arc on the horizon, typically, those colors include, to varying degrees, red, orange, yellow, green, blue, indigo, violet.

5. According to the United States Constitution, **impeachment** of a president, which is an accusation of criminal activity, is initiated by the House of Representatives, and conviction occurs in the Senate by two-thirds majority, once convicted, the president is removed from office.

ACTIVITY 7: CORRECTING SENTENCE BOUNDARY PROBLEMS

Comma splices and run-on problems happen when a writer fails to show a clear boundary between two sentences. Match the two sentences. Then, to prevent a comma splice or run-on, do one of the following: (1) make two sentences, (2) use a semicolon, or (3) add a comma plus *and, but, or, for, so, yet*. Use each of the three ways at least once.

First Sentence	Next Sentence
1. I'm not someone who likes to talk a lot about myself, or thinks I'm any big deal Bethany Hamilton, *Soul Surfer*	a. occasionally, on a rare and magic day, a white winter sun broke through
2. You don't think of fear as a factor in professional football Michael Lewis, *The Blind Side*	b. you assume that the sort of people who make it to the NFL are **immune** [*resistant*] to the emotion
3. Gerry loves the fall and hates the heat Anna Quindlen, *Lots of Candles, Plenty of Cake*	c. my family saw something in my story that would be helpful and interesting to others and encouraged me to write it down
4. Like most dogs of his breed he drooled a little Sterling North, *Rascal*	d. I prefer summer and am **sanguine** [*okay*] about humidity
5. Usually it was fog in January in Holland, dank, chill, and gray Corrie ten Boom, *The Hiding Place*	e. in the house he had to lie with his muzzle on a bath towel, his eyes downcast as though in slight disgrace

ACTIVITY 8: FIXING SENTENCE BOUNDARY PROBLEMS

Read each item and then use the letter from this list to describe it:

a. comma splice problem

b. run-on problem

c. both problems

d. no problem

Next, revise any item that contains a comma splice, a run-on, or both problems.

1. Because Egyptians believed in an afterlife, they were concerned about what that life would be like one Egyptian book had spells to protect people from being forced to walk upside-down.

2. Manatees, which are large sea mammals, can stay submerged for up to twenty minutes, this happens only when they are rested.

3. The highest number of wild cat species ever recorded in one place is seven, a forest in India holds that record.

4. A dairy cow produces enough milk in her lifetime to make nine thousand gallons of ice cream, which people eat more of on Sunday than any other day of the week, probably because Sunday is usually not a workday.

5. Half of all animal and plant species live in the rain forest, only around six percent of the earth's land surface is rain forest that's an amazing fact.

6. A pudu, found in South America, is the world's smallest deer, standing only a maximum of seventeen inches, they have antlers that shed annually they **protrude** [*reach*] from between their ears up to three inches.

7. The rain forest **canopy** [*covering*] is so thick that a raindrop does not penetrate immediately to the ground, taking up to ten minutes as a result the canopy is covered with standing water until penetration occurs.

8. Each of the *Star Wars* movies made over 400 million worldwide, the top earner was not the first film but the sequel titled *The Phantom Menace*, grossing 924 million worldwide.

9. In 1963, in Paris, France, author Pierre Boulle published *La Planete des Singes*, translated that same year as *The Planet of the Apes* in the United States, it was translated in 1964 as *Monkey Planet* in the United Kingdom.

10. Stinkhorn, which is a type of fungi in rain forests, gets its name from its horrible odor, smelling like garbage.

YOUR TURN: PROOFREADING

Pretend you work as a proofreader for a publisher. A proofreader's job is to search writing to locate problems, including comma splices and run-ons. Your editor assigned you to correct the passages below, filled with those problems. Capital letters and periods—the usual markers for the beginning and the ending of a sentence—are missing.

DIRECTIONS

1. Copy each passage while adding capital letters and periods to mark sentence boundaries. When you finish, you should have the number of sentences indicated.

2. Exchange your work with other students in your class to achieve agreement on the correct sentence boundaries. Discuss any discrepancies until you and they agree on the correct sentence boundaries.

PASSAGE ONE *(Seven Sentences)*:
Lincoln's Assassin at Lincoln's Inauguration

It looked like a bad day for photographers terrible winds and thunderstorms had swept through Washington early that morning, dissolving the dirt streets into a sticky muck of soil and garbage the ugly gray sky of the morning of March 4, 1865 threatened to spoil the great day close to the Capitol, Alexander Gardner set up his camera to photograph the inauguration he captured not only images of the president, vice president, chief justice, and other honored guests occupying the stands, but also the anonymous faces of hundreds of spectators who crowded the east front of the Capitol in one photograph, on a balcony above the stands, a young man with a black mustache and wearing a top hat gazes down on the president it is the famous actor John Wilkes Booth, subsequently Lincoln's assassin.

James L. Swanson, *Chasing Lincoln's Killer*

PASSAGE TWO (*Ten Sentences*):
The Building of the Amazing Ship Titanic

To build the *Titanic* took almost three years its owner, the White Star
Line, had spared no expense in making this the best ship afloat when
all the work was done, the Titanic had cost more than $10 million,
which was a mind-boggling amount back in 1912 from front to back
the *Titanic* measured 882 feet, almost as long as three football fields
the steel plates of the *Titanic* were held in place by more than 3 million
metal rivets the rivets alone weighed 1,200 tons the ship's mammoth
rudder was as tall as a house, and weighed a hundred tons the *Titanic*
had three giant propellers, powered by steam engines as strong as
46,000 horses as long as four city blocks and as tall as an eleven-story
building, the *Titanic* was incredible for its first voyage, the ship was
scheduled to travel from Southampton, England, to New York, but the
Titanic never made it to New York.

Thomas Conklin, *The Titanic Sinks!*

PASSAGE THREE (*Thirteen Sentences*):
A Little Girl's Dress Catches on Fire

I was on fire it's my earliest memory I was three years old I was
standing on a chair in front of the stove, wearing a pink dress my
grandmother had bought for me the dress's skirt stuck out like a tutu,
and I liked to spin around in front of the mirror, thinking I looked like
a ballerina at that moment, I was wearing the dress to cook hot dogs
Juju, our black mutt, was watching me I stabbed one of the hot dogs
with a fork and bent over and offered it to him when I stood up and
started stirring the hot dogs again I felt a blaze of heat on my right
side I turned to see where it was coming from and realized my dress
was on fire frozen with fear, I watched the yellow-white flames make a

ragged brown line up the pink fabric of my skirt and climb my stomach then the flames leaped up, reaching my face I screamed I smelled the burning and heard a horrible crackling as the fire singed my hair and eyelashes.

Jeannette Walls, *The Glass Castle: A Memoir*

REMARKABLE EVENTS: FASCINATING DETAILS

Right now, you are going to learn how the sentences in a model paragraph by an author are built, and then write an imitation paragraph with your sentences built pretty much the same way.

You'll learn about remarkable events, mainly little-known details surrounding an historical event. For example, within the American Civil War there were snowball fights between the soldiers for their entertainment. You've heard the saying "Truth is stranger than fiction." In the remarkable events below, you'll see that "Nonfiction is stranger than fiction."

IMITATING PARAGRAPHS ABOUT REMARKABLE EVENTS

When you imitate the model paragraphs, which are short nonfiction excerpts, you will succeed if you focus on these goals:

Blueprint for Paragraph—Build your sentences like those in the model. The sentence structure of the model paragraph is a blueprint for your paragraph.

Material for Paragraph—Tell something remarkable your readers don't already know. For example, if the general topic is the American Civil War, it's not remarkable that soldiers fought with weapons; it is remarkable that in winter, to pass the time, they had snowball fights.

Benefits of Paragraph—Write paragraphs with two benefits for your readers: information and entertainment. In your paragraphs, pretend you are a writer for a magazine that features fascinating glimpses into history that are tidbits your readers will enjoy.

ACTIVITY 1: BUILDING THE EIFFEL TOWER

One of architecture's most remarkable feats, the tower rapidly became a worldwide phenomenon, among the most famous structures in modern history.

*During its construction, even as the tower pushed towards the clouds, a chorus of opposing voices rose in protest, attacking it as a meaningless gesture, **devoid** [empty] of **function** [purpose], and too **reminiscent** [suggestive] of an industrial smokestack.*

—Lucien Herve, *The Eiffel Tower*

OBSERVING EQUIVALENT SENTENCE STRUCTURE

Study the model paragraph and its imitation with equivalent sentence structure. To see the similarity in sentence structure, read the first sentence from each paragraph, then the second, then the third, and so forth.

MODEL PARAGRAPH

(1) Gustave Eiffel **relentlessly** [*continually*] pushed to ensure [guarantee] that his tower would be built by May 1889. (2) A self-made millionaire, France's most successful railway bridge builder, and an engineer of **global** [*worldwide*] ambition, Eiffel had company offices in Peru, Saigon, Shanghai. (3) Stolid and imperturbable, he could be found most days directing his workers as they assembled the colossal wrought-iron tower. (4) For nine months, Parisians watched in fascination as the slanting legs of the much-discussed structure rose. (5) The many who hated Eiffel's tower felt quite **vindicated** [*justified*] because the partially built tower looked like an ugly, **hulking** [*massive*] creature.

Jill Jones, *Eiffel's Tower* (adapted)

IMITATION PARAGRAPH

(1) The Eiffel Tower magnificently stands to verify that its namesake would be remembered by future generations. (2) An iron lattice structure, a global cultural icon of France, and an image of instant recognition, the Tower has two main levels with spectacular views, sit-down restaurants, and elevators. (3) Breathtaking but controversial, the Tower was unmistakably visible, marking the entrance when the 1889 World's Fair opened its gates. (4) Since its beginning, the Tower amazes without end as the international crowds with stories to remember visit. (5) The tourists who gape at the Eiffel Tower number in the millions because the third-level view looks out on stunning, romantic Paris.

IMITATING THE MODEL PARAGRAPH

Choose another remarkable event, learn more about that event online or offline, and then write an imitation of the model paragraph above about the Eiffel Tower. Build your sentences in a similar way, but fill them with information about your topic. Choose one of these topics, or one of your own:

- discovering electricity
- walking across Niagara Falls on a tightrope
- developing the Internet
- building the Panama Canal.

The sentences from both the model paragraph and its imitation are broken down below into their sentence parts to help you focus on how each part is built. Imitate each sentence part, one at a time, to write sentences for your paragraph like the sentences in the model paragraph. Your imitation doesn't have to be exact, just approximate, built pretty much like the model.

Model	Imitation
1a. Gustave Eiffel relentlessly pushed	**1a.** The Eiffel Tower magnificently stands
1b. to ensure that his tower	**1b.** to verify that its namesake
1c. would be built by May 1889.	**1c.** would be remembered by future generations.
2a. A self-made millionaire,	**2a.** An iron lattice structure,
2b. France's most successful railway bridge builder,	**2b.** a global cultural icon of France,
2c. and an engineer of global ambition,	**2c.** and an image of instant recognition,
2d. Eiffel had company offices	**2d.** the Tower has two main levels
2e. in Peru, Saigon, Shanghai.	**2e.** with spectacular views, sit-down restaurants, and elevators.
3a. Stolid and imperturbable,	**3a.** Breathtaking but controversial,
3b. he could be found most days	**3b.** the Tower was unmistakably visible,
3c. directing his workers	**3c.** marking the entrance
3d. as they assembled the colossal wrought-iron tower.	**3d.** when the 1889 World's Fair opened its gates.
4a. For nine months,	**4a.** Since its beginning,
4b. Parisians watched in fascination	**4b.** the Tower amazes without end
4c. as the slanting legs	**4c.** as the international crowds
4d. of the much-discussed structure	**4d.** with eyes in awe
4e. rose.	**4e.** visit.
5a. The many	**5a.** The tourists
5b. who hated Eiffel's tower	**5b.** who gape at the Eiffel Tower
5c. felt quite vindicated	**5c.** number in the millions
5d. because the partially built tower	**5d.** because the third-level view
5e. looked like an ugly, hulking creature.	**5e.** looks out on stunning, romantic Paris.

ACTIVITY 2: SINKING OF THE *TITANIC*

On its very first voyage, the *Titanic*, the largest ship at the time, considered unsinkable, collided with an iceberg April 15, 1912, in the North Atlantic and sank. In one of the worst disasters on sea ever, over 1,500 persons died, most of them freezing to death from the subfreezing temperature of the water.

OBSERVING EQUIVALENT SENTENCE STRUCTURE

Study the model paragraph and its imitation with equivalent sentence structure. To see the similarity in sentence structure, read the first sentence from each paragraph, then the second, then the third, and so forth.

MODEL PARAGRAPH

(1) Thanks to the great fanfare that surrounded its launching, the *Titanic* carried many celebrities. (2) There was real estate tycoon John Astor IV, the richest man in America, returning from honeymoon with his wife, who would give birth to their child four months after saying goodbye to her husband on the *Titanic*. (3) The great British socialite Lady Lucy Duff Gordon, famed for her Lucy range of **boutiques** [*shops*], was traveling to New York with her husband, the Olympic sportsman Sir Cosmo Duff Gordon. (4) They were traveling **incognito** [*unidentified*] to avoid the attention of the press. (5) Millionaire industrialist Benjamin Guggenheim, plus the co-founder of Macy's department store Isidor Straus, as well as various actors, politicians, and titled **gentry** [*wealthy*] were also passengers.

Nic Compton, *Titanic on Trial* (adapted)

IMITATION PARAGRAPH

(1) Because of the huge prestige that attached to working on the *Titanic*, the ship boasted many experts. (2) It was the second of three

Olympic class ocean liners, the largest ship afloat in the ocean, sailing from Southampton, England to New York City with 2,224 passengers and crew, 1,500 of whom would die during the crossing four days into the voyage after the collision with the iceberg. (3) The renowned naval architect Thomas Andrews, aboard for the *Titanic's* maiden voyage, was lost in the tragic sinking, the deadliest peacetime maritime disaster in modern history. (4) The ship had been built painstakingly to handle any problem during the trip. (5) Experienced Captain Edward Smith plus a crew of hundreds as well as various waiters, maids, and kitchen help were also onboard.

IMITATING THE MODEL PARAGRAPH

Choose another remarkable event, learn more about that event online or offline, and then write an imitation of the model paragraph above about the sinking of the *Titanic*. Build your sentences in a similar way, but fill them with information about your topic. Choose one of these topics, or one of your own:

- experiencing the 2004 Asian tsunami
- landing on the Moon by Apollo 11 in 1969
- attempting to climb Mt. Everest
- invading Normandy in World War II.

The sentences from both the model paragraph and its imitation are broken down below into their sentence parts to help you focus on how each part is built. Imitate each sentence part, one at a time, to write sentences for your paragraph like the sentences in the model paragraph. Your imitation doesn't have to be exact, just approximate, built pretty much like the model.

Model	Imitation
1a. Thanks to the great fanfare **1b.** that surrounded its launching, **1c.** the Titanic carried many celebrities.	**1a.** Because of the huge prestige **1b.** that attached to working on the *Titanic*, **1c.** the ship boasted many experts.
2a. There was real estate tycoon John Astor IV, **2b.** the richest man in America, **2c.** returning from honeymoon with his wife, **2d.** who would give birth to their child **2e.** four months after saying goodbye **2f.** to her husband on the *Titanic*.	**2a.** It was the second of three Olympic class ocean liners, **2b.** the largest ship afloat in the ocean, **2c.** sailing from Southampton, England to New York City with 2,224 passengers and crew, **2d.** 1,500 of whom would die during the crossing **2e.** four days into the voyage **2f.** after she hit an iceberg.
3a. The great British socialite Lady Lucy Duff Gordon, **3b.** famed for her Lucy range of boutiques, **3c.** was traveling to New York with her husband, **3d.** the Olympic sportsman Sir Cosmo Duff Gordon.	**3a.** The renowned naval architect Thomas Andrews, **3b.** aboard for the *Titanic's* maiden voyage, **3c.** was lost in the tragic sinking, **3d.** the deadliest peacetime maritime disaster in modern history.
4a. They were traveling incognito **4b.** to avoid the attention of the press.	**4a.** The ship had been built painstakingly **4b.** to handle any problem during the trip.
5a. Millionaire industrialist Benjamin Guggenheim **5b.** plus the co-founder of Macy's department store Isidor Straus, **5c.** as well as various actors, politicians, and titled gentry **5d.** were also passengers.	**5a.** Experienced Captain Edward Smith **5b.** plus a crew of hundreds **5c.** as well as various waiters, maids, and kitchen help **5d.** were also onboard.

ACTIVITY 3: WITNESSING HOUDINI'S AMAZING TRICKS

The greatest magician and escape artist the world has ever seen, Harry Houdini amazed thousands throughout the world with his tricks. He considered himself indestructible. Once he challenged a man to hit him hard and repeatedly in his stomach, claiming he'd remain unharmed. Houdini died days later from complications of the blows to his stomach.

OBSERVING EQUIVALENT SENTENCE STRUCTURE

Study the model paragraph and its imitation with equivalent sentence structure. To see the similarity in sentence structure, read the first sentence from each paragraph, then the second, then the third, and so forth.

MODEL PARAGRAPH

(1) Houdini walked through a red-brick wall, and came through without a scratch. (2) Houdini clapped his hands like cymbals and made a five-ton elephant disappear. (3) Tightly strapped and buckled into a canvas straitjacket designed to **restrain** [*control*] the violently insane, he was raised by his ankles to dangle like a fish from the edge of a tall building. (4) He wriggled free as **adroitly** [*skillfully*] as a moth emerges from a cocoon. (5) Crowned the king of handcuffs, Houdini, **shackled** [*bound*] at his wrists and ankles, was nailed into a wooden packing case and thrown into the waters of New York Harbor. (6) Moments later, he splashed to the surface, rattling **aloft** [*overhead*] the police jewelry. (7) Houdini escaped the inescapable.

Sid Fleischman, *Escape: The Story of the Great Houdini* (adapted)

IMITATION PARAGRAPH

(1) Houdini escaped from commissioned handcuffs, and broke through after an hour's struggle. (2) He buried himself in another trick but

barely escaped with his life. (3) Completely upsidedown and chained inside a locked glass cabinet made to hold massive water, Houdini was able for three minutes to hold his breath within the cabinet in this most famous of all his acts. (4) He gained wiggle room as cleverly as a mouse escapes from a cat. (5) Able to enlarge his shoulders and chest, Houdini, imprisoned inside this locked cabinet, was saved by an exhalation of breath and emerged from his trap to an amazed audience. (6) After this, he dislocated his shoulders, escaping from a straitjacket. (7) Houdini fooled the unfoolable.

IMITATING THE MODEL PARAGRAPH

Choose another remarkable event, learn more about that event online or offline, and then write an imitation of the model paragraph above about Houdini. Build your sentences in a similar way, but fill them with information about your topic. Choose one of these topics, or one of your own:

- writing of the national anthem, "Star-Spangled Banner"
- killing of John Lennon
- experiencing Hurricane Katrina
- winning one for the Gipper (Notre Dame football coach).

The sentences from both the model paragraph and its imitation are broken down below into their sentence parts to help you focus on how each part is built. Imitate each sentence part, one at a time, to write sentences for your paragraph like the sentences in the model paragraph. Your imitation doesn't have to be exact, just approximate, built pretty much like the model.

Model	Imitation
1a. Houdini walked through a red-brick wall, **1b.** and came through **1c.** without a scratch.	**1a.** Houdini escaped from commissioned handcuffs, **1b.** and broke through **1c.** after an hour's struggle.
2a. Houdini clapped his hands **2b.** like cymbals **2c.** and made a five-ton elephant disappear.	**2a.** He buried himself **2b.** in another trick **2c.** but barely escaped with his life.
3a. Tightly strapped and buckled into a canvas straitjacket **3b.** designed to restrain the violently insane, **3c.** he was raised by his ankles **3d.** to dangle like a fish **3e.** from the edge of a tall building.	**3a.** Completely upside-down and chained inside a locked glass cabinet **3b.** made to hold massive water, **3c.** Houdini was able for three minutes **3d.** to hold his breath within the cabinet **3e.** in this most famous of all his acts.
4a. He wriggled free **4b.** as adroitly as **4c.** a moth emerges from a cocoon.	**4a.** He gained wiggle room **4b.** as cleverly as **4c.** a mouse escapes from a cat.
5a. Crowned the king of handcuffs, **5b.** Houdini, **5c.** shackled at his wrists and ankles, **5d.** was nailed into a wooden packing case **5e.** and thrown into the waters of New York Harbor.	**5a.** Able to enlarge his shoulders and chest, **5b.** Houdini, **5c.** imprisoned inside this locked cabinet, **5d.** was saved by an exhalation of breath **5e.** and emerged from his trap to an amazed audience.
6a. Moments later, **6b.** he splashed to the surface, **6c.** rattling aloft the police jewelry.	**6a.** After this, **6b.** he dislocated his shoulders, **6c.** escaping from a straitjacket.
7a. Houdini **7b.** escaped the inescapable.	**7a.** Houdini **7b.** fooled the unfoolable.

ACTIVITY 4: ATTACKING THE UNITED STATES ON SEPTEMBER 11, 2001

Four terrorist suicide attacks occurred on that infamous date, using hijacked passenger planes as weapons to fly into intended targets. One crashed into a field in Pennsylvania after passengers intervened and stopped the plan. A second plane hit the Pentagon in Washington, D.C., and the two others hit the twin towers of the World Trade Center in New York City, where almost 3,500 people, including firefighters and police, were killed.

OBSERVING EQUIVALENT SENTENCE STRUCTURE

Study the model paragraph and its imitation with equivalent sentence structure. To see the similarity in sentence structure, read the first sentence from each paragraph, then the second, then the third, and so forth.

MODEL PARAGRAPH

(1) On September 11, 2001, in an office on Lower Manhattan high in the North Tower of the World Trade Center, a data processor glanced up from his computer. (2) On the horizon, a dot in the sky got his attention. (3) Moments later, from his **perch** [*place*] on a structure, a steelworker was startled by a sight and the roar of an airliner flying so low that it almost hit the antenna of the Empire State Building. (4) On a nearby corner, construction workers stared in astonishment. (5) Seated in a restaurant window, a composer heard a jet thunder overhead. (6) Pigeons, normally calm, rose in alarm. (7) A student gazing out a window at his high school on the banks of the Hudson River glimpsed the plane and screamed. (8) In the North Tower of the World Trade Center, the data processor, who had seen the plane as a distant dot, was not looking when it came right at him.

Anthony Summers and Robbyn Swan, *The 11th Day* (adapted)

IMITATION PARAGRAPH

(1) On that tragic day in a financial center of the United States deep in the Manhattan borough of New York City, one terrorist attack went down as an unspeakable horror. (2) From fourteen terrorists, four coordinated attacks on America brought catastrophe. (3) Months earlier, about several Islamic outposts in the Middle East, Osama bin Laden had been upset by Americans in Saudi Arabia and the impact of American sanctions threatening Iraq so strongly that America clearly angered the terrorist component of al-Qaeda. (4) Over a Pennsylvania field, United Airlines flight 93 passengers overcame the hijackers. (5) Prevented by the passengers, the attempt missed the terrorists' intended objective. (6) The second President Bush, urgently informed, reacted in shock. (7) Some passengers hijacked by a group of al-Qaeda terrorists with the aim of destroying four targets understood the plan and reacted. (8) In three targets of four planned attacks, the terrorists, who had intended mass destruction as their goal, were succeeding when they crashed the commandeered planes.

IMITATING THE MODEL PARAGRAPH

Choose another remarkable event, learn more about that event online or offline, and then write an imitation of the model paragraph above about September 11, 2001. Build your sentences in a similar way, but fill them with information about your topic. Choose one of these topics, or one of your own:

- inventing refrigeration for food
- tracing the disappearance of Amelia Earhart
- describing the voyage of the Kon-Tiki raft
- creating Mickey Mouse.

The sentences from both the model paragraph and its imitation are broken down below into their sentence parts to help you focus on how each part is built. Imitate each sentence part, one at a time, to write sentences for your paragraph like the sentences in the model paragraph. Your imitation doesn't have to be exact, just approximate, built pretty much like the model.

Model	Imitation
1a. On September 11, 2001, **1b.** in an office on Lower Manhattan **1c.** high in the North Tower of the World Trade Center, **1d.** a data processor **1e.** glanced up from his computer.	**1a.** On that tragic day **1b.** in a financial center of the United States **1c.** deep in the Manhattan borough of New York City, **1d.** one terrorist attack **1e.** went down as an unspeakable horror.
2a. On the horizon, **2b.** a dot in the sky **2c.** got his attention.	**2a.** From fourteen terrorists, **2b.** four coordinated attacks on America **2c.** brought catastrophe.
3a. Moments later, **3b.** from his perch on a structure, **3c.** a steelworker **3d.** was startled by a sight **3e.** and the roar of an airliner **3f.** flying so low that it almost hit **3g.** the antenna of the Empire State Building.	**3a.** Months earlier, **3b.** about several Islamic outposts in the Middle East, **3c.** Osama bin Laden **3d.** had been upset by Americans in Saudi Arabia **3e.** and the impact of American sanctions **3f.** threatening Iraq so strongly that America clearly angered **3g.** the terrorist component of al-Qaeda.
4a. On a nearby corner, **4b.** construction workers **4c.** stared in astonishment.	**4a.** Over a Pennsylvania field, **4b.** United Airlines flight 93 passengers **4c.** overcame the hijackers.

5a. Seated in a restaurant widow, **5b.** a composer **5c.** heard a jet thunder overhead.	**5a.** Prevented by the passengers, **5b.** the attempt **5c.** missed the terrorists' intended objective.
6a. Pigeons, **6b.** normally calm, **6c.** rose in alarm.	**6a.** The second President Bush, **6b.** urgently informed, **6c.** reacted in shock.
7a. A student **7b.** gazing out a window at his high school **7c.** on the banks of the Hudson River **7d.** glimpsed the plane **7e.** and screamed.	**7a.** Some passengers **7b.** hijacked by a cadre of al-Qaeda terrorists **7c.** with the aim of destroying four targets **7d.** understood the plan **7e.** and reacted.
8a. In the North Tower **8b.** of the World Trade Center, **8c.** the data processor, **8d.** who had seen the plane as a distant dot, **8e.** was not looking when it came right at him.	**8a.** In three targets **8b.** of four planned attacks, **8c.** the terrorists, **8d.** who had intended mass destruction as their goal, **8e.** were not failing when they crashed the commandeered planes.

ACTIVITY 5: ENTERTAINING THE CIVIL WAR SOLDIERS

During lulls in the fighting, Civil War soldiers, although the war was grim and deadly, found ways to entertain themselves.

Winter was a respite from the horror of the Civil War, and the passage below describes the lives of these soldiers camped in Virginia in the brief, quiet interlude between the terrifying battles of 1862 and 1863.

—S. C. Gwynne, *Rebel Yell*

OBSERVING EQUIVALENT SENTENCE STRUCTURE

Study the model paragraph and its imitation with equivalent sentence structure. To see the similarity in sentence structure, read the first sentence from each paragraph, then the second, then the third, and so forth.

MODEL PARAGRAPH

(1) Probably the most fun the soldiers had that winter were the snowball fights. (2) Many of them had never seen snow before. (3) Now there was lots of it, and they knew just what to do. (4) Every time it snowed, there were battles, usually involving small groups of soldiers. (5) On at least one occasion, they mounted a fight on a massive scale. (6) Two armies were formed of 2,500 men each, complete with authentic generals, colors, signal corps, fifers, and drummers announcing the coming attack. (7) They conducted head-on assaults and flank attacks. (8) According to reports, it was probably the greatest snowball battle ever fought. (9) Robert E. Lee, who came out to observe the battle, was struck by several snowballs.

S. C. Gwynne, *Rebel Yell* (adapted)

IMITATION PARAGRAPH

(1) Interestingly, the most useful thing the soldiers built that winter was a clapboard theatre. (2) Most of them had never acted before. (3) Now there were scripts for plays, and they liked performing for fellow soldiers. (4) Every night they gathered there were farces, often making fun of their officers. (5) In one of the funnier skits, doctors amputated a head with a rusty saw. (6) The soldier was presented with a fake headless body, shown with soldier's uniform, bloody bandages, dangling legs, weapon, and a horse carrying the headless body. (7) Soldiers enjoyed satiric portrayals and funny skits. (8) Entertaining the troops, the programs were certainly the most appreciated theatrical performances ever presented. (9) One madcap soldier who came out and completely undressed was cheered by the entirely male audience.

IMITATING THE MODEL PARAGRAPH

Choose another remarkable event, learn more about it online or offline, and then write an imitation of the nine-sentence model paragraph about snowball fights during the American Civil War. Build your sentences in a similar way, but fill them with information about your topic. Choose one of these topics, or one of your own:

- building the pyramids
- discovering Atlantis
- killing Osama bin Laden
- landing Apollo 11 on the moon
- constructing One World Trade Center in New York City.

The sentences from both the model paragraph and its imitation are broken down below into their sentence parts to help you focus on how each part is built. Imitate each sentence part, one at a time, to write sentences for your paragraph like the sentences in the model paragraph. Your imitation doesn't have to be exact, just approximate, built pretty much like the model.

Model	Imitation
1a. Probably **1b.** the most fun the soldiers had that winter **1c.** were the snowball fights.	**1a.** Interestingly **1b.** the most useful thing the soldiers built that winter **1c.** was a clapboard theatre.
2a. Many of them **2b.** had never seen snow before.	**2a.** Most of them **2b.** had never acted before.
3a. Now there was lots of it, **3b.** and they knew just what to do.	**3a.** Now there were scripts for plays, **3b.** and they liked performing for fellow soldiers.

4a. Every time it snowed, **4b.** there were battles, **4c.** usually involving small groups of soldiers.	**4a.** Every night they gathered **4b.** there were farces, **4c.** often making fun of their officers.
5a. On at least one occasion **5b.** they mounted a fight **5c.** on a massive scale.	**5a.** In one of the funnier skits, **5b.** doctors amputated a head **5c.** with a rusty saw.
6a. Two armies were formed **6b.** of 2,500 men each, **6c.** complete with authentic generals, colors, signal corps, fifers, **6d.** and drummers announcing the coming attack.	**6a.** The soldier was presented **6b.** with a fake headless body, **6c.** shown with soldier's uniform, bloody bandages, dangling legs, weapon, **6d.** and a horse carrying the headless body.
7a. They conducted **7b.** head-on assaults and flank attacks.	**7a.** Soldiers enjoyed **7b.** satiric portrayals and funny skits.
8a. According to reports, **8b.** it was probably **8c.** the greatest snowball battle ever fought.	**8a.** Entertaining the troops, **8b.** the programs were certainly **8c.** the most appreciated theatrical performances ever presented.
9a. Robert E. Lee, **9b.** who came out to observe the battle, **9c.** was struck by several snowballs.	**9a.** One madcap soldier **9b.** who came out and completely undressed **9c.** was cheered by the entirely male audience.

SCULPTING SENTENCES

Italian artist Michelangelo, who sculpted famous statues like *David* and *Pieta*, carved those amazing works from blocks of stone. He believed that the stone held captive a statue but that the sculptor, using vision, creativity, and skill, could free the statue from its stone prison. In the following activities, you'll sculpt sentences about remarkable events with information from a list of ordinary sentences. Create sentences like ones by authors—sentences comparable to a sculptor's stone waiting to be shaped into something great—to build paragraphs like those of an author.

Sculpting sentences isn't just combining the listed sentences but adding or removing words, tweaking wording, varying structures, and more—anything that would build a strong sentence like one by an author.

Every block of stone has a statue inside it,
and it is the task of the sculptor to discover it.
I saw the angel in the marble and carved until I set him free.

—Michelangelo

ACTIVITY 6: GLIMPSING THE BLACK DEATH

In fourteenth-century Europe, the worst plague in history struck, killing with remarkable speed, resulting in death often within 24 hours of infection. During a three-year period, twenty-five million people perished, one-half of Europe's population. Because of the black spots that appeared on the skin of its victims, the plague was called the Black Death.

The Black Death produced suffering and death on a scale
that, even after two world wars and twenty-seven million
deaths worldwide from AIDS, remains astonishing.

—John Kelly, *The Great Mortality*

Directions: Sculpt the ordinary sentences into a paragraph *with four sentences.*

Sculpt the following information into the <u>first sentence</u> of your paragraph.

1a. The Black Death affected every country in Europe.

1b. It probably began as an endemic.

1c. An endemic is a locally confined disease.

1d. Once that disease is established it is **perpetually** [*always*] present.

Sculpt the following information into the <u>second sentence</u> of your paragraph.

2a. Flea, rodent, or human populations spread the disease elsewhere.

2b. This happened through faster, more efficient trade or communications networks.

2c. When this occurred, the disease became a pandemic.

2d. A pandemic is a widespread disease.

Sculpt the following information into the <u>third sentence</u> of your paragraph.

3a. The far-flung Mongol Empire was established in the East.

3b. It linked Asia to Europe in an overland network.

3c. The network included mounted armies, postal carriers, and caravans.

Sculpt the following information into the <u>fourth sentence</u> of your paragraph.

4a. The disease was **transmitted** [*spread*] from its endemic centers in the East.

4b. Then the plague easily made its way across Europe.

4c. This happened through well-established **trade** [*business*] routes.

(adapted from John Aberth, The Black Death)

ACTIVITY 7: CONSUMING TELEVISION

Television in America quickly became a means of instantaneous, widespread communication, and a pervasive consumer of hours of a person's daily life.

The typical person in the United States watches television approximately 4 hours each day, and will spend nine full years in front of a TV set by age sixty-five. Comparable numbers for their children are destined to be higher, and don't include hours spent consuming other old and new media as well.

—Gary Edgerton, *The Columbia History of American Television*

Directions: Sculpt the ordinary sentences into a paragraph *with five sentences.*

Sculpt the following information into the <u>first sentence</u> of your paragraph.

1a. This happened centuries ago.

1b. Information and imagery moved only so far and fast.

1c. This was because people had to carry them.

Sculpt the following information into the <u>second sentence</u> of your paragraph.

2a. This happens today.

2b. Digital language of instant communication is everywhere.

2c. This is mostly by television and computers.

2d. Together, they number over one billion units in America alone.

Sculpt the following information into the <u>third sentence</u> of your paragraph.

3a. America has **profoundly** [*greatly*] changed.

3b. It has redefined how people conduct several things.

3c. These things are their home life, work, and leisure.

3d. It has also redefined how they understand the image-saturated world.

3e. These changes in American lives are largely a result of television.

Sculpt the following information into the <u>fourth sentence</u> of your paragraph.

4a. Television integrated fast into American life.

4b. No technology before TV ever integrated faster.

Sculpt the following information into the <u>fifth sentence</u> of your paragraph.

5a. Television took only ten years.

5b. Then ten years was what it took to reach penetration.

5c. The penetration was thirty-five million households.

5d. The telephone required eighty years.

5e. The automobile required fifty years.

5f. The radio required twenty-five years.

(adapted from Gary Edgerton,
The Columbia History of American Television)

ACTIVITY 8: SWIMMING THE ENGLISH CHANNEL

Although many men and women had tried and failed, only five men succeeded in swimming the twenty-one-mile turbulent and dangerous, shark-infested waterway connecting France to England. In 1926, Gertrude "Trudy" Ederle, a nineteen-year-old American Olympic swimmer, was the first woman to succeed. America was completely smitten by Trudy and cheered her on to ultimate success.

The great Channel refused to be taken easily by anyone, whether in great ships or a simple swimsuit. The thought of a woman doing it seemed **preposterous** [impossible] *to many, especially a teenager who couldn't understand the difficulties she would face.*

—Tim Dahlberg, Mary Ederle Ward, and Brenda Green,
*America's Girl: The Incredible Story of How Swimmer
Gertrude Ederle Changed the Nation*

Directions: Sculpt the ordinary sentences into a paragraph *with six sentences.*

Sculpt the following information into the first sentence of your paragraph.

1a. A few men managed to swim across the English Channel.

1b. There were a dozen who failed for every one who succeeded.

Sculpt the following information into the second sentence of your paragraph.

2a. The swimmers were usually **slathered** [*covered*] in grease.

2b. This was done to ward off the cold water.

2c. The swim was such a marathon.

2d. The elements usually won.

Sculpt the following information into the <u>third sentence</u> of your paragraph.

3a. If the elements didn't win, the masses of jellyfish picked off the rest.

3b. The jellyfish had bites that were both painful and poisonous.

Sculpt the following information into the <u>fourth sentence</u> of your paragraph.

4a. If any woman had a chance, it was Trudy Ederle.

4b. She was nineteen years old.

4c. She had a shy yet **engaging** [*charming*] smile.

4d. She had broad shoulders.

Sculpt the following information into the <u>fifth sentence</u> of your paragraph.

5a. She spent her summers at the beach.

5b. She loved to swim in the ocean.

5c. She had been smashing world records since the age of fifteen.

Sculpt the following information into the <u>sixth sentence</u> of your paragraph.

6a. America was **captivated** [*charmed*].

6b. Trudy captivated it.

Tim Dahlberg, Mary Ederle Ward, and Brenda Green,
*America's Girl: The Incredible Story of How Swimmer
Gertrude Ederle Changed the Nation* (adapted)

ACTIVITY 9: LEARNING ABOUT THE FIRST EMAIL

Before the invention of the telegraph, written communication was very far from instantaneous. The Pony Express, a procedure to deliver written mail via riders on horseback, was used to send letters, but delivery could take as long as ten days and require a change of riders every seventy-five miles and horses every fifteen miles to reach its recipient. The telegram, which was the first email, required neither riders nor horses to deliver the same letter almost instantaneously via the telegraph.

---

*The Western Union company became synonymous with the word telegram. That company built the nation's first transcontinental telegraph line in 1861. By the end of the century, the company was **transmitting** [sending] 58 million telegraphed messages per year.*

—Linda Rosenkrantz, *Telegram*

Directions: Sculpt the ordinary sentences into a paragraph *with eight sentences*.

Sculpt the following information into the <u>first sentence</u> of your paragraph.

1a. The telegraph was valuable.

1b. Its value was demonstrated during the Civil War.

1c. Strands of wire were strung on **makeshift** [*temporary*] poles.

1d. The poles were throughout the fields of the countryside.

1e. These poles allowed for the **instantaneous** [*immediate*] communication of military intelligence.

Sculpt the following information into the second sentence of your paragraph.

2a. The telegraph was also a **key** [*important*] factor in the development of two things.

2b. One of them was the commercial life in the United States.

2c. The other was social life in the United States.

2d. This development of the two things happened in **succeeding** [*following*] decades.

Sculpt the following information into the third sentence of your paragraph.

3a. The telegraph led to many accomplishments.

3b. Among the many accomplishments was the **transmission** [*sending*] of news.

3c. The transmission was instant.

3d. It was **via** [*through*] press wire services.

Sculpt the following information into the fourth sentence of your paragraph.

4a. The telegraph speeded up something else.

4b. It speeded up the very pace of life.

4c. The life was daily.

Sculpt the following information into the fifth sentence of your paragraph.

5a. The impact of the telegraph was great.

5b. This was true particularly in the second half of the nineteenth century.

5c. The impact was as great as the impact of the printing press.

5d. The printing press happened some 400 years before.

Sculpt the following information into the <u>sixth sentence</u> of your paragraph.

6a. The telegraph was the technological revolution.

6b. That revolution was essentially the first stop.

6c. The stop was on the information superhighway.

Sculpt the following information into the <u>seventh sentence</u> of your paragraph.

7a. Telegraphy allowed individuals to transmit words.

7b. The transmission was in a new way.

7c. It sped declarations of eternal love.

7d. It also sped desperate **pleas** [*requests*] for money in emergencies.

7e. It also sped news of life from the **remotest** [*farthest*] rural areas to **urban** [*city*] centers.

7f. These centers were thousands of miles away.

Sculpt the following information into the <u>eighth sentence</u> of your paragraph.

8a. The telegram had urgency.

8b. The urgency was impossible to ignore.

8c. The urgency was impossible to set aside.

8d. The urgency was impossible to dump into an electronic trash can.

8e. The trash can is the one in our own day with email.

(adapted from Linda Rosenkrantz, Telegram)

Directions: In the next part, you are not given a sentence-by-sentence breakdown. Sculpt the list of ordinary sentences into the indicated number of sentences in the original paragraph.

ACTIVITY 10: ASSASSINATING ABRAHAM LINCOLN

Perhaps because of the carelessness of his bodyguard the night of his assassination, Lincoln was killed.

Even before he took the oath of office, Abraham Lincoln was the object of plots to kidnap or kill him. Throughout the Civil War he received threatening letters. Finally, late in the war, he agreed to allow four Washington police officers to act as his bodyguards.

—Ronald Kessler, *In the President's Secret Service*

Directions: Sculpt the ordinary sentences into a paragraph with *no more than six sentences.*

1. This event happened on April 14, 1865.
2. John Wilkes Booth learned that Lincoln would be attending a play.
3. Booth was a **fanatical** [*radical*] Confederate **sympathizer** [*ally*].
4. The play was at Ford's Theatre that evening.
5. President Lincoln's bodyguard was Patrolman John F. Parker.
6. He was on duty that night.
7. He was a member of the Washington police.
8. Parker wandered off instead of remaining on guard outside the president's box.
9. The box was inside the theatre.
10. He wandered elsewhere to watch the play.
11. Then he went to a nearby **saloon** [*bar*] for a drink.
12. Park's **negligence** [*carelessness*] left Lincoln unprotected.

13. Lincoln was as unprotected as any private citizen.

14. Booth made his way to Lincoln's box.

15. This happened just before 10 P.M.

16. He snuck in.

17. He shot Lincoln in the back of the head.

18. Lincoln died.

19. His death occurred the next morning.

(adapted from Ronald Kessler, *In the President's Secret Service*)

ACTIVITY 11: HANGING INNOCENT PEOPLE AS WITCHES

The infamous Salem witchcraft trials of women and men accused in colonial Massachusetts in June 1692 resulted in the death sentences of innocent people. The horrible accusations of innocent people resulted from a mistaken belief that some people were witches. The accusers and the accused were heard in courts set up to hear the cases, but unfortunately twenty innocent people were executed.

By October 1692 so many improbable candidates had been named as witches that the public grew skeptical. For all its drama, the witch hunt flared and fizzled in under a year. The Massachusetts government admitted its terrible mistake in 1697, paying restitution to the victims' families.

—Diane Foulds, *Death in Salem*

Directions: Sculpt the ordinary sentences into a paragraph *with no more than ten sentences.*

1. The witch hunt started in a home.

2. It was the home of the Reverend Samuel Parris.

3. His nine-year-old daughter and twelve-year-old niece **dabbled** [*played*] in fortune-telling.

4. The girls dropped a raw egg.

5. They dropped it into a glass of water.

6. They wanted to reveal their future husbands.

7. An **image** [*picture*] of a coffin seemed to appear.

8. This was a horrifying **omen** [*sign*].

9. The girls suffered a breakdown.

10. The local doctor found their breakdown **mystifying** [*mysterious*].

11. He **attributed** [*assigned*] their condition to witchcraft.

12. Panic spread to other households.

13. Twenty persons were put to death.

14. Their deaths happened within eleven months.

15. The **contagion** [*infection*] **engulfed** [*swallowed*] at least twenty-two villages.

16. The villages were in Massachusetts.

17. The **culmination** [*result*] was the arrest of accused people.

18. There were arrests of over one hundred fifty people.

19. Fifty-nine were tried.

20. Thirty-one were convicted.

21. Nineteen were hung.

22. Much of the testimony drew upon **spectral** [*insubstantial*] evidence.

23. There were **impassioned** [*emotional*] claims.

24. The claims were that the accused were witches.

25. The **alleged** [*accused*] witches were sending their spirits out to **wreak** [*cause*] mischief.

26. This mischief was on **hapless** [*unfortunate*] innocents.

27. Most of the suspects admitted to the crime.

28. They did this because confessors were not as likely to be hanged.

29. There was one stubborn old man.

30. His name was Giles Corey.

31. He was accused.

32. He refused to stand trial.

33. He was pressed to death because of his refusal.

34. Pressing was a torture.

35. It consisted of placing heavier and heavier stones upon someone's chest.

36. This continued until the person pleaded innocent or guilty, or died.

(adapted from Diane Foulds, *Death in Salem*)

ACTIVITY 12: KNOCKING TEETH OUT

In ancient times, people suffering toothaches were exposed to primitive treatments, in contrast to the treatments of modern dentistry. Removing a painful tooth created more pain than the toothache itself.

Sixty-five hundred years ago, one of our Neolithic ancestors had a toothache. His tooth had cracked down the center and the top had rotted out, leaving the sensitive pulp exposed. Every time something hot or cold touched the pulp, an agonizing electric shock of pain racked his body.

—Jim Murphy, "This Won't Hurt a Bit" in *Guys Read: True Stories*

Directions: Sculpt the ordinary sentences into a paragraph *with no more than ten sentences.*

1. Sometimes the pain became horrible.
2. It was so horrible that the sufferer begged for relief.
3. A stick was used.
4. It was used to remove the tooth.
5. It was placed against the side of the **offending** [*hurting*] tooth.
6. It was hit with a rock or a hammer.
7. It took a few solid whacks.
8. That would get the job done.
9. **Cost-efficient** [*thrifty*] dentists used their fingers.
10. They used their fingers to wiggle the tooth loose.
11. These dentists were in ancient Japan.
12. The increase in tooth **extractions** [*removals*] might have had a result.
13. This result might very well have been a new job.
14. The new job was because a dental assistant was required.
15. The assistant was required to hold the patient down.

16. The patient was held down as his or her tooth was knocked out.

17. Two countries showed a creative **streak** [*characteristic*].

18. These countries were ancient Greece and ancient Rome.

19. The streak happened when it came to getting teeth out of a patient's mouth.

20. Hippocrates described an advanced tooth-pulling **device** [*tool*] found in Greece.

21. He was known as the father of Western medicine.

22. This happened around 400 B.C.

23. The device was a metal instrument.

24. It resembled an oversize pair of **forceps** [*tweezers*].

25. The dentist would clamp the tip around the bad tooth.

26. Then the dentist would wiggle it out.

27. He would do this without any sort of painkiller.

28. There was a young dentist named Celsus.

29. He lived around A.D. 10 in ancient Rome.

30. Celsus came up with a new way to remove a rotten tooth's roots.

31. He cut the gum away from around the tooth.

32. He pulled the skin free to expose the tooth.

33. This was also without painkillers.

34. The tooth would then be **extracted** [*removed*].

35. The extraction would use either the fingers or forceps.

(adapted from Jim Murphy, "This Won't Hurt a Bit"
in *Guys Read: True Stories*)

YOUR TURN: VIGNETTE

Without imitating an author's paragraph but writing a paragraph so good it could have been written by an author, write a vignette about a remarkable event. A vignette is a brief but interesting description or episode.

Directions:

1. Select one of the topics below—or choose one of your own.

SPORTS RECORDS

- Barry Bonds (baseball)
- Wilt Chamberlain (basketball)
- Jackie Joyner-Kersee (track and field)
- Jesse Owens (track and field)
- Michael Phelps (swimming)

BATTLES

- Lexington and Concord (1775)
- Waterloo (1815)
- Gettysburg (1863)
- Guadalcanal (1942–43)
- Tet Offensive (1968)

MAN-MADE DISASTERS

- Love Canal at Niagara Falls (1940)
- Three Mile Island nuclear meltdown (1979)
- Union Carbide gas leak in India (1984)

- Exxon Valdon oil spill (1989)
- nuclear power plant explosion in Chernobyl, Russia (1989)

SCIENTIFIC DISCOVERIES

- DNA
- gravity
- pasteurization
- penicillin
- X-rays

SPACE EXPLORATION

- Yuri Gargarin reaching outer space
- *Apollo 8* circling the moon
- *Apollo 11* humans walking on the moon
- *Salyut 1* establishing the first space station
- *Challenger* breaking apart

INVENTIONS

- airplane
- automobile
- calculator
- computer
- eyeglasses

2. Learn more about your remarkable event online or offline, and then draft and revise a one-paragraph vignette about that event.

3. Pretend you are a writer for a magazine that features compellingly interesting vignettes. Your job is to write an informative vignette about some aspect of the remarkable event.

4. Create a one-paragraph vignette that readers will believe was written by an author. Use a variety of sentence-composing tools in various positions: *openers*, *S-V splits*, *closers*. (See the following student sample titled "Gold" for examples.)

5. Exchange your draft with other students in your class for suggestions to improve your paragraph, and give them suggestions, too. Then revise several times until your paragraph is finished.

6. Create a memorable title that your readers won't understand until after they read your paragraph. *Example:* "Space Walker," a title for a vignette about Alexei Leonov, the first person to walk in outer space.

REVIEW

SENTENCE-COMPOSING TOOLS

Before drafting your vignette, study Peter's student paragraph about a remarkable sporting event: Michael Phelps winning the most gold medals in Olympic history.

Notice Peter's use of sentence-composing tools in varied positions—*openers*, *S-V splits*, *closers*:

- openers *italicized* (*pages 48–54*)

- S-V splits <u>underlined</u> (*pages 55–61*)

- closers **bolded** (*pages 62–68*).

"Gold"
by
Peter Maleki
(*a student paper*)

(1) *Once unrecognized by many people*, he used to be a nobody, **a young man so unknown that he might as well have never existed**. (2) It wasn't until the 2008 Olympics that he became one of the most widely recognized athletes in the world. (3) He won eight consecutive gold medals in one Olympic season, **an achievement unprecedented in the history of the Olympics**. (4) He is Michael Phelps, **a native of Baltimore, Maryland who began his career very early in his life**. (5) *A ten-year-old boy diagnosed with attention-deficit hyperactivity disorder*, Michael, his mind unable to stay focused in school, discovered his natural talent as a swimmer, **holding the national records for his age group**. (6) *At the remarkable age of fifteen*, Michael qualified for the Olympics, **the youngest age for a male qualifying as an Olympic swimmer in over sixty-eight years**. (7) *A teenager fifteen and nine months*, he had broken the world record for the 200-meter butterfly, **becoming the youngest man ever to set a swimming record**. (8) *Having won many medals in various events in the 2004 Olympics including six gold medals*, he entered Beijing for the 2008 Olympics. (9) Michael, trying so hard to do well, had no idea that he would go on to win eight gold medals, **the record for the most gold medals won by anyone for a single event in the Olympics**. (10) *His goal to win unwavering, his determination solid*, he competed unflinchingly, **winning one gold medal after another**, **an astonishing and unprecedented achievement**. (11) He won them all, **eighteen gold medals, the most gold in Olympic history**. (12) Michael Phelps, Olympian gold-medalist unexcelled, became a worldwide Olympic superstar. (13) There may never again be another Olympic champion receiving more global and golden acclaim.

SENTENCE-BY-SENTENCE ANALYSIS

To appreciate the power of Peter's use of sentence-composing tools in various positions, focus below on the before and after use of tools in Peter's vignette. Tools are bolded.

Sentence 1 contains an opener and a closer.

Before Tools: He used to be a nobody.
After Tools: **Once unrecognized by many people**, he used to be a nobody, **a young man so unknown that he might as well have never existed**.

Sentence 2 contains no tools.

Sentence 3 contains a closer.

Before Tools: He won eight consecutive gold medals in one Olympic season.
After Tools: He won eight consecutive gold medals in one Olympic season, **an achievement unprecedented in the history of the Olympics**.

Sentence 4 contains a closer.

Before Tools: His name is Michael Phelps.
After Tools: His name is Michael Phelps, **a native of Baltimore, Maryland who began his career very early in his life**.

Sentence 5 contains all three positions—an opener, an S-V split, and a closer.

Before Tools: Michael discovered his natural talent as a swimmer.
After Tools: **A ten-year-old boy diagnosed with attention-deficit hyperactivity disorder**, Michael, **his mind unable to stay focused in school**, discovered his natural talent as a swimmer, **holding the national records for his age group**.

Sentence 6 contains an opener and a closer.

Before Tools: Michael qualified for the Olympics.

After Tools: **At the remarkable age of fifteen,** Michael qualified for the Olympics, **the youngest age for a male qualifying as an Olympic swimmer in over sixty-eight years**.

Sentence 7 contains an opener and a closer.

Before Tools: He had broken the world record for the 200-meter butterfly.
After Tools: **A teenager fifteen and nine months,** he had broken the world record for the 200-meter butterfly, **becoming the youngest man ever to set a swimming record.**

Sentence 8 contains an opener.

Before Tools: He entered Beijing for the 2008 Olympics.
After Tools: **Having won many medals in various events in the 2004 Olympics including six gold medals,** he entered Beijing for the 2008 Olympics.

Sentence 9 contains an S-V split and a closer.

Before Tools: Michael had no idea that he would go on to win eight gold medals.
After Tools: Michael, **trying so hard to do well,** had no idea that he would go on to win eight gold medals, **the record for the most gold medals won by anyone for a single event in the Olympics**.

Sentence 10 contains an opener and two closers.

Before Tools: He competed unflinchingly.
After Tools: **His goal to win unwavering, his determination solid,** he competed unflinchingly, **winning one gold medal after another, an astonishing and unprecedented achievement.**

Sentence 11 contains two closers.

Before Tools: He won them all.
After Tools: He won them all, **nineteen medals, the most gold in Olympic history.**

Sentence 12 contains an S-V split.

Before Tools: Michael Phelps became a worldwide Olympic superstar.
After Tools: Michael Phelps, **Olympian gold-medalist unexcelled**, became a worldwide Olympic superstar.

Sentence 13 contains no tools.

Using tools like *openers, S-V splits, closers* builds better sentences—thick not thin, long not short, packed not empty—in and beyond middle school, and for college or career.

ANALYZING SENTENCES

Observing the side-by-side contrast above, list five or more verifiable conclusions supported by Peter's use of the sentence-composing tools in various positions.

EXAMPLES

- Most sentences except sentence 2 contain at least one sentence-composing tool (eleven out of thirteen).

- Peter uses more than one place in almost half of his sentences (six out of thirteen).

  BUILDING SENTENCES LIKE AN AUTHOR: After drafting your vignette about a remarkable event, revise it to be sure that it contains sentences built with sentence-composing tools in various positions: *openers, S-V splits, closers.*

REMARKABLE PLACES: STRANGE BUT TRUE

Learn about places that have attracted people, including places shrouded in mystery, places considered a world wonder, places remarkable because of their uniqueness or strangeness.

In this section, activities focus on paragraphs from informational text, especially details and facts associated with these remarkable places. You'll learn how the sentences in a model nonfiction paragraph are built, and then imitate that model paragraph by building your sentences like those.

When you write your paragraphs about remarkable places, your content can come from your current knowledge, or new knowledge from online or offline searches.

IMITATING PARAGRAPHS ABOUT REMARKABLE PLACES

Writer for Paragraph—Pretend you are a writer for a paper or digital magazine featuring interesting but little-known info about remarkable places—appetizing tidbits your readers will enjoy.

Material for Paragraph—Tell something interesting your readers don't already know about the remarkable place.

Blueprint for Paragraph—Build your sentences like those in the model paragraph, which is a blueprint for your paragraph about a remarkable place.

ACTIVITY 1: POMPEII

In Italy, near the city of Naples, is Mount Vesuvius, which erupted in 79 A.D. in history's most infamous volcano. In the catastrophe, the volcano sent stones, fumes, and ash twenty miles high, throwing 1.5 million tons of rock per second, burying the nearby town of Pompeii, and resulting in tremendous loss of life and countless injuries.

*Because of its **exceptional** [unusual] state of preservation under volcanic ash, Pompeii has provided excavators **intimate** [close] views into the life of an ancient civilization. With its intact streets, its graffiti, shops, temples, houses, gardens, paintings, statues, and its **poignant** [sad] traces of the disaster's victims, human and animal, the buried city has captured the imagination of generations of visitors, readers, and moviegoers.*

—Ingrid D. Rowland, *From Pompeii*

SAME SENTENCE STRUCTURE

Read the model paragraph and then the imitation paragraph with sentences built the same way. To see the similarity in sentence structure, read the first sentence from each paragraph, then the next sentence, then the next, and so forth.

MODEL PARAGRAPH

(1) Archaeologists have recovered traces of more than a thousand victims of the volcanic eruption that destroyed Pompeii, including a poor dog straining at its leash, and a group of three hundred people stranded on the seashore, waiting for evacuation by sea. (2) The actual toll of the disaster must have numbered nearly 16,000, with many thousands more injured. (3) By the end of the **cataclysm** [*disaster*], the volcano's **profile** [*appearance*] had changed **radically** [*greatly*], from a graceful, conical peak to a jagged crater, created when the force of the eruption of Mount Vesuvius blew the top off the mountain.

Ingrid D. Rowland, *From Pompeii* (adapted)

IMITATION PARAGRAPH

(1) Historians have reported ships of the Imperial Navy near the erupting volcano that attempted rescue, crossing the turbulent bay hoping for surviving victims, and a number of other possible survivors spotted on another shore, hoping for rescue by boat. (2) The unfortunate people of Pompeii were covered in 12 layers of ash, with all buildings also ashen. (3) In the force of the eruption, Pompeii's citizens had died quickly, from a traveling hot surge of 250 degree centigrade, peaking when the temperature of the blast of the volcano killed many victims from the heat.

IMITATING THE MODEL PARAGRAPH

First, learn online or offline about one of these other remarkable places:

- Times Square, New York City, United States—*neon, flashy hub of the City*

- Lotte World, Seoul, Korea—*world's largest indoor theme park*

- Louvre Museum, Paris, France—*most visited museum in the world*

- Forbidden City, Beijing, China—*home to many Chinese emperors*

- Disney World, Orlando, Florida, United States—*amusement park with the Magic Kingdom.*

Then, using that place, practice building sentences like those of an author by writing an imitation of the three-sentence model paragraph.

The sentences from both the model paragraph and its imitation are broken down below into their sentence parts to help you focus on how each part is built. Imitate each sentence part, one at a time, to write sentences for your paragraph like the sentences in the model paragraph. Your imitation doesn't have to be exact, just approximate, built pretty much like the model.

Model	Imitation
1a. Archaeologists have recovered	**1a.** Historians have reported
1b. traces of more than a thousand victims	**1b.** ships of the imperial navy
1c. of the volcanic eruption	**1c.** near the erupting volcano
1d. that destroyed Pompeii,	**1d.** that attempted rescue,
1e. including a poor dog	**1e.** crossing the turbulent bay
1f. straining at its leash,	**1f.** hoping for surviving victims,
1g. and a group of three hundred people	**1g.** and a number of other possible survivors
1h. stranded on the seashore,	**1h.** spotted on another shore,
1i. waiting for evacuation by sea.	**1i.** hoping for rescue by boat.
2a. The actual toll of the disaster	**2a.** The unfortunate people of Pompeii
2b. must have numbered nearly16,000,	**2b.** were covered in twelve layers of ash,
2c. with many thousands more injured.	**2c.** with all buildings also ashen.
3a. By the end of the cataclysm,	**3a.** In the force of the eruption,
3b. the volcano's profile	**3b.** Pompeii's citizens
3c. had changed radically,	**3c.** had died quickly,
3d. from a graceful, conical peak	**3d.** from a traveling hot surge
3e. to a jagged crater,	**3e.** of 250 degree centigrade,
3f. created when the force of the eruption of Mount Vesuvius	**3f.** peaking when the temperature of the blast of the volcano
3g. blew the top off the mountain.	**3g.** killed many victims from the heat.

ACTIVITY 2: BERMUDA TRIANGLE

The triangle is an area of 500,000 miles bounded by Miami, Puerto Rico, and Bermuda where planes and ships have mysteriously disappeared. Theorists speculate that the cause could be aliens, sea monsters, even time warps and reverse gravity fields. Scientists think the cause, found elsewhere with similar disappearances, could be magnetic anomalies, waterspouts, or huge eruptions of methane gas from the ocean floor.

*This is the area commonly called the Bermuda Triangle. In the **annals** [records] of sea mysteries there is no other place that challenges mankind with so many extraordinary and **incredible** [unbelievable] events, for that is where far more aircraft and ships have disappeared than in any other region of the world's oceans.*

—Gian J. Quasar, *Into the Bermuda Triangle*

SAME SENTENCE STRUCTURE

Read the model paragraph and then the imitation paragraph with sentences built the same way. To see the similarity in sentence structure, read the first sentence from each paragraph, then the next sentence, then the next, and so forth.

MODEL PARAGRAPH

(1) Many of the planes simply vanished while in sight of land, while coming in for a landing, or after having just departed, occurring between a single sweep of the radarscope. (2) Others vanished over shallow waters less than 10 feet deep, with equal lack of radar trace or **silhouette** [*shadow*] to mark their position. (3) Magically, they just faded away, while others vanished during radio contact. (4) At the edge of the harbor, missing boats vanished, others while cruising around a peninsula, and others found drifting, lifeless, the occupants gone without leaving any **clue** [*sign*] of what happened.

Gian J. Quasar, *Into the Bermuda Triangle: Pursuing the Truth Behind the World's Greatest Mystery* (adapted)

IMITATION PARAGRAPH

(1) A squadron of five bombers abruptly disappeared after being in range of radar, while forming a basic training triangle, and after having left Ft. Lauderdale, vanishing after several radio communications from the crew. (2) Their pilots excelled in flying missions always with complete confidence, with high credentials of 350 flight hours and experience to mark their qualifications. (3) Mysteriously, all five planes just disappeared abruptly, while others faded into nonexistence. (4) In the stories of the Triangle, strange explanations flourished, some while suggesting connections to Atlantis, and others seemed mysterious, bizarre, the disappearances happening without showing a trace of what occurred.

IMITATING THE MODEL PARAGRAPH

First, learn online or offline about one of these other remarkable places:

- Ocean Park, Hong Kong, China—*home of Hong Kong's biggest roller coaster, plus a huge maritime mammal park*

- Sydney Opera House, Sydney, Australia—*group of linked buildings housing one of the world's largest and busiest arts centers*

- Zocalo, Mexico City, Mexico—*area of one of the largest main squares and gathering places in the world*

- Central Park, New York City, United States—*green oasis in the heart of the city featuring sports and entertainment events*

- Grand Bazaar, Istanbul, Turkey—*immense outdoor market selling varied special products within its fifteenth-century vaulted walkways*

Then, using that place, practice building sentences like those of an author by writing an imitation of the four-sentence model paragraph.

The sentences from both the model paragraph and its imitation are broken down below into their sentence parts to help you focus on how each part is built. Imitate each sentence part, one at a time, to write sentences for your paragraph like the sentences in the model paragraph. Your imitation doesn't have to be exact, just approximate, built pretty much like the model.

Model	Imitation
1a. Many of the planes simply vanished	**1a.** A squadron of five bombers abruptly disappeared
1b. while in sight of land,	**1b.** after being in range of radar,
1c. while coming in for a landing,	**1c.** while forming a basic training triangle,
1d. or after having just departed,	**1d.** and after having left Ft. Lauderdale,
1e. occurring between a single sweep of the radarscope.	**1e.** vanishing after several radio communications from the crew.
2a. Others vanished over shallow waters	**2a.** Their pilots excelled in flying missions
2b. less than 10 feet deep,	**2b.** always with complete confidence,
2c. with equal lack of radar trace	**2c.** with high credentials of 350 flight hours
2d. or silhouette	**2d.** and experience
2e. to mark their position.	**2e.** to mark their qualifications.
3a. Magically,	**3a.** Mysteriously,
3b. they just faded away,	**3b.** all five planes just disappeared abruptly,
3c. while others vanished during radio contact.	**3c.** while others faded into virtual nonexistence.
4a. At the edge of the harbor,	**4a.** In the stories of the Triangle,
4b. missing boats vanished,	**4b.** strange explanations flourished,
4c. others while cruising around a peninsula,	**4c.** some while suggesting connections to Atlantis,
4d. and others were found drifting,	**4d.** and others seemed mysterious,
4e. lifeless,	**4e.** bizarre,
4f. the occupants gone	**4f.** the disappearances happening
4g. without leaving any clue	**4g.** without showing a trace
4h. of what happened.	**4h.** of what occurred.

ACTIVITY 3: AMSTERDAM

One-quarter of Amsterdam's surface is water, making it the most watery city in the world, containing a network of man-made canals that, during its Golden Age in the 1700s, made Amsterdam the busiest and wealthiest port in the world.

> *The Dutch Republic had so many interconnected canals*
> *that water transport became the preferred mode of travel.*
> *During a cold winter, an energetic youth much like*
> *the fabled Hans Brinker could actually skate from*
> *one city to another on the country's extensive*
> *network of frozen canals.*
>
> —Deborah Davis, *Fabritius and the Goldfinch*

SAME SENTENCE STRUCTURE

Read the model paragraph and then the imitation paragraph with sentences built the same way. To see the similarity in sentence structure, read the first sentence from each paragraph, then the next sentence, then the next, and so forth.

MODEL PARAGRAPH

(1) Amsterdam started out as a giant swamp, with large expanses of land below sea level and subject to flooding. (2) Over the years, experts approached the problem with great **ingenuity** [*originality*], concluding that the best way to prevent flooding was to contain the water and its power with a system of canals and dikes. (3) In 1609 a group of businessmen funded an experiment to reclaim underwater land. (4) **Hydraulics** [*water*] engineers created the country's first land **reclaimed** [*saved*] from water, building a dike around a large lake,

digging a canal, and using pumps powered by windmills to **siphon** [*transfer*] the water into the canal. (5) The project was such a success that its investors ended up with dry land that was fertile, **habitable** [*livable*], and immensely beautiful.

Deborah Davis, *Fabritius and the Goldfinch* (adapted)

IMITATION PARAGRAPH

(1) Amsterdam once was the wealthiest city in the world with valuable exports of products of great variety and intended for North America. (2) During that time, merchants expanded their trade with growing interest, realizing that the profitable way to invest money was to create a company and a network through the start of businesses and markets. (3) In 1602 the Amsterdam office of the Dutch East India Company created the world's first stock exchange to trade its shares. (4) Amsterdam merchants held the most shares bought from companies, dictating the products sold to buyers, enjoying the large profits, and creating trade routes designed by veterans to transport merchandise across the world. (5) Their golden age earned such wealth that Amsterdam became the world's center that was cultured, envied, and clearly magnetic.

IMITATING THE MODEL PARAGRAPH

First, learn online or offline about one of these other remarkable places:

- Glacier Skywalk, Jasper National Park, Canadian Rockies, Canada— *thrilling glass walkway 918 feet above the ground for an unobstructed view downward*

- One World Trade Center, New York City, United States— *replacement for the buildings destroyed in a terrorist attack and tallest building in Western Hemisphere*

- Cinecitta World, Rome, Italy—*first theme park in the eternal city, featuring movie-related attractions and rides*

- National Air and Space Museum, Washington, D.C., United States—*largest collection of aircraft and spacecraft in the world*

- Tate Museum, London, United Kingdom—*world's most popular and largest collection of modern art.*

Then, using that place, practice building sentences like those of an author by writing an imitation of the five-sentence model paragraph.

The sentences from both the model paragraph and its imitation are broken down below into their sentence parts to help you focus on how each part is built. Imitate each sentence part, one at a time, to write sentences for your paragraph like the sentences in the model paragraph. Your imitation doesn't have to be exact, just approximate, built pretty much like the model.

Model	Imitation
1a. Amsterdam started out as a giant peat swamp,	**1a.** Amsterdam once was the wealthiest city in the world
1b. with large expanses of land below sea level	**1b.** with valuable exports of products of great variety
1c. and subject to flooding.	**1c.** and intended for North America.
2a. Over the years,	**2a.** During that time,
2b. experts approached the problem with great ingenuity,	**2b.** merchants expanded their trade with growing interest,
2c. concluding that the best way to prevent flooding	**2c.** realizing that the profitable way to invest money
2d. was to contain the water and its power	**2d.** was to create a company and a network
2e. with a system of canals and dikes.	**2e.** through the start of businesses and markets.

3a. In 1609 **3b.** a group of businessmen funded an experiment **3c.** to reclaim underwater land.	**3a.** In 1602 **3b.** the Amsterdam office of the Dutch East India Company created the world's first stock exchange **3c.** to trade its shares.
4a. Hydraulics engineers created the country's first land reclaimed from water, **4b.** building a dike around a large lake, **4c.** digging a ring canal, **4d.** and using pumps powered by windmills **4e.** to siphon the water into the canal.	**4a.** Amsterdam merchants held the most shares bought from companies, **4b.** dictating the products sold to buyers, **4c.** enjoying the large profits, **4d.** and creating trade routes designed by veterans **4e.** to transport merchandise across the world.
5a. The project was such a success **5b.** that its investors ended up with dry land **5c.** that was fertile, habitable, and immensely beautiful.	**5a.** Their golden age earned such wealth **5b.** that Amsterdam became the world's center **5c.** that was cultured, envied, and clearly magnetic.

ACTIVITY 4: NIAGARA FALLS

Niagara Falls is the name for the three falls on the Canadian/United States border. Since 1901, when teacher Annie Taylor went over the Falls in a wooden barrel, emerging with only minor cuts, daredevils have attempted either tightrope walking over the falls or plunging over them within some kind of container, sometimes resulting in their deaths, obviously ignoring Annie's advice: "No one ought ever to do that again."

The Niagara has always been dangerous. Boating accidents and drowning have claimed an untold number of lives. The death and mayhem that distinguish the Niagara from other rivers occur in a six-mile stretch of water that may best be described as hungry.

—T. W. Kriner, *In the Mad Water*

SAME SENTENCE STRUCTURE

Read the model paragraph and then the imitation paragraph with sentences built the same way. To see the similarity in sentence structure, read the first sentence from each paragraph, then the next sentence, then the next, and so forth.

MODEL PARAGRAPH

(1) Any boater unfortunate enough to pass from the broad, calm river into the churning water rapids below it is unlikely to survive. (2) At that point the river takes a downhill turn, dropping some sixty feet in half a mile. (3) This slope is sufficient to turn the river into a seething hell of white water. (4) As it tumbles downhill, the river accelerates to nearly twenty-five miles per hour, then plunges into an ancient gorge over three distinct **cataracts** [*waterfalls*] known **collectively** [*together*] as Niagara Falls. (5) The drop from the surface of the river above to the surface of the river in the gorge below is about one hundred eighty feet. (6) Approximately three hundred tons of water each second pass over their **brinks** [*edges*].

T. W. Kriner, *In the Mad Water* (adapted)

IMITATION PARAGRAPH

(1) A sixty-three-year-old teacher first to plunge over the Falls' treacherous edge with only a barrel around her body was lucky to succeed. (2) With that first stunt the Falls took on an allure, beckoning

daredevils around the world. (3) Niagara Falls is famous enough to transform any comer into an instant celebrity of fleeting fame. (4) Since the teacher's historic feat, others have tried with barrels or other containers, often descending the steepest Fall with an outside shot risked stupidly like a gambler. (5) One daredevil in a steel barrel for the descent to the bottom of the Falls in the river there finished with broken kneecaps and jaw. (6) Occasionally more thrill seekers within various contraptions go over the Falls.

IMITATING THE MODEL PARAGRAPH

First, learn online or offline about one of these other remarkable places:

- Lincoln Memorial, Washington, D.C., United States—*monument honoring the sixteenth president of the United States*

- Everland, Gyeonggi-Do, South Korea—*home to the world's steepest wooden roller coaster, plus a zoo and a water park*

- Victoria Peak, Hong Kong, China—*highest mountain in Hong Kong with breathtaking views of the city*

- Great Pyramid, El Giza, Egypt—*last of the seven wonders of the ancient world still standing*

- Taj Mahal, Agra, India—*jewel of Muslim art in India and regarded as one of the world's architectural masterpieces.*

Then, using that place, practice building sentences like those of an author by writing an imitation of the six-sentence model paragraph.

The sentences from both the model paragraph and its imitation are broken down below into their sentence parts to help you focus on how each part is built. Imitate each sentence part, one at a time, to write sentences for your paragraph like the sentences in the model paragraph. Your imitation doesn't have to be exact, just approximate, built pretty much like the model.

Model	Imitation
1a. Any boater unfortunate enough **1b.** to pass from the broad, calm river **1c.** into the churning water rapids below it **1d.** is unlikely to survive.	**1a.** A sixty-three-year-old teacher first **1b.** to plunge over the Falls' treacherous edge **1c.** with only a barrel around her body **1d.** was lucky to succeed.
2a. At that point **2b.** the river takes a downhill turn, **2c.** dropping some sixty feet in half a mile.	**2a.** With that first stunt **2b.** the Falls took on an allure, **2c.** beckoning daredevils around the world.
3a. This slope is sufficient **3b.** to turn the river **3c.** into a seething hell of white water.	**3a.** Niagara Falls is famous enough **3b.** to transform any comer **3c.** into an instant celebrity of fleeting fame.
4a. As it tumbles downhill, **4b.** the river accelerates **4c.** to nearly twenty-five miles per hour, **4d.** then plunges into an ancient gorge **4e.** over three distinct cataracts **4f.** known collectively as Niagara Falls.	**4a.** Since the teacher's historic feat, **4b.** others have tried **4c.** with barrels or other containers, **4d.** often descending the steepest Fall **4e.** with an outside shot **4f.** risked stupidly like a gambler.
5a. The drop **5b.** from the surface of the river above **5c.** to the surface of the river in the gorge below **5d.** is about one hundred eighty feet.	**5a.** One daredevil **5b.** in a steel barrel for the descent **5c.** to the bottom of the Falls in the river there **5d.** finished with broken kneecaps and jaw.
6a. Approximately three hundred tons of water each second **6b.** pass over their brinks.	**6a.** Occasionally more thrill seekers inside various contraptions **6b.** go over the Falls.

ACTIVITY 5: PANAMA CANAL

More than forty years in the making, this waterway links the Atlantic and Pacific Oceans, allowing ships to avoid a much longer trip to go from one ocean to the other. An expedition of the United States Navy led by Isaac

Strain attempted the process. He and a party of twenty-seven men—six of whom died from starvation—were among the first to attempt to trace a land path from the Atlantic Ocean to the Pacific Ocean. What happened represents the struggles of many to find a path between the two seas that, many years later, became the Panama Canal.

The creation of the Panama Canal represented, apart from wars, the largest, most costly single effort ever before mounted anywhere on earth. It held the world's attention over a span of forty years. It affected the lives of tens of thousands of people at every level of society and of virtually every race and nationality.

—David McCullough, *The Path Between the Seas: The Creation of the Panama Canal 1870–1914*

SAME SENTENCE STRUCTURE

Read the model paragraph and then the imitation paragraph with sentences built the same way. To see the similarity in sentence structure, read the first sentence from each paragraph, then the next sentence, then the next, and so forth.

MODEL PARAGRAPH

(1) Verging on starvation, the men **devoured** [*ate*] anything they could lay hands on, including live toads and a variety of palm nut that burned the enamel from their teeth and caused **excruciating** [*painful*] stomach cramps. (2) The smothering heat, the rains, the **forbidding** [*fearful*] jungle twilight were unlike anything any of them had ever experienced. (3) Seven men died. (4) That any survived was due mainly to Strain's

extraordinary **fortitude** [*strength*]. (5) Torn, bleeding, and virtually naked, Strain, after finding help from an Indian village, turned around and led a rescue mission back to save the others. (6) Later, a doctor described the survivors as living skeletons, covered with foul ulcers, most weighing under seventy-five pounds.

David McCullough, *The Path Between the Seas:*
The Creation of the Panama Canal 1870–1914 (adapted)

IMITATION PARAGRAPH

(1) Struggling with climate, the French suffered enormous work force problems they could not control, including malaria and a virulent yellow fever that cost the project thousands of lives and caused increasing financial problems. (2) The rainy weather, the heat, the unforeseen mortality rate were not factors any of the French engineers had planned on. (3) The United States took over. (4) That the project succeeded was due mostly to America's engineering expertise. (5) Determined, courageous, and newly encouraged, America, after assessing the situation in the Canal Zone, persevered anyway and created a more friendly environment to promote workers' health. (6) Afterward, observers described the infrastructure as hospitable buildings, designed with incoming workers in mind, most coming from America.

IMITATING THE MODEL PARAGRAPH

First, learn online or offline about one of these other remarkable places:

- Nazca Desert, Peru—*site of enormous ancient drawings of mysterious origin on land*

- Ice Hotel, Jukkasjarvi, Sweden—*hotel constructed of ice and snow and rebuilt each year*

- Leap Castle, Roscrea, Ireland—*reportedly the most haunted castle in the world*

- Varosha, Famagusta, Cyprus—*completely uninhabited abandoned resort town on the coast of Cyprus*

- Mont St. Michel, Normandy, France—*famous landmark island protected during high tide from attacking armies.*

Then, using that place, practice building sentences like those of an author by writing an imitation of the six-sentence model paragraph.

The sentences from both the model paragraph and its imitation are broken down below into their sentence parts to help you focus on how each part is built. Imitate each sentence part, one at a time, to write sentences for your paragraph like the sentences in the model paragraph. Your imitation doesn't have to be exact, just approximate, built pretty much like the model.

Model	Imitation
1a. Verging on starvation,	**1a.** Struggling with climate,
1b. the men devoured anything they could lay hands on,	**1b.** the French suffered enormous work force problems they could not control,
1c. including live toads	**1c.** including malaria
1d. and a variety of palm nut	**1d.** and a virulent yellow fever
1e. that burned the enamel from their teeth	**1e.** that cost the project thousands of lives
1f. and caused excruciating stomach cramps.	**1f.** and caused increasing financial problems.
2a. The smothering heat, the rains, the forbidding jungle twilight	**2a.** The rainy weather, the heat, the unforeseen mortality rate
2b. were unlike anything	**2b.** were not factors
2c. any of them had ever experienced.	**2c.** any of the French engineers had planned on.
3a. Seven men	**3a.** The United States
3b. died.	**3b.** took over.

4a. That any survived **4b.** was due mainly **4c.** to Strain's extraordinary fortitude.	**4a.** That the project succeeded **4b.** was due mostly **4c.** to America's engineering expertise.
5a. Torn, bleeding, and virtually naked, **5b.** Strain, **5c.** after finding help from an Indian village, **5d.** turned around **5e.** and led a rescue mission back **5f.** to save the others.	**5a.** Determined, courageous, and newly encouraged, **5b.** America, **5c.** after assessing the situation in the Canal Zone, **5d.** persevered anyway **5e.** and created a more friendly environment **5f.** to promote workers' health.
6a. Later, **6b.** a doctor described the survivors **6c.** as living skeletons, **6d.** covered with foul ulcers, **6e.** most weighing under seventy-five pounds.	**6a.** Afterward, **6b.** observers described the infrastructure **6c.** as hospitable buildings, **6d.** designed with incoming workers in mind, **6e.** most coming from America.

SCULPTING SENTENCES

Each list of basic sentences in the next activities contains information about a remarkable place—sentences comparable to a sculptor's stone waiting to be shaped by the sculptor into something great. Using that information, write a paragraph containing sentences built like those of an author. Here's your challenge: sculpt superb sentences out of that block of stone.

ACTIVITY 6: MOUNT EVEREST

In the Himalayan mountain range, Mount Everest is Earth's highest mountain, 29,029 feet above sea level. Because of the thin atmosphere, most climbers need supplemental oxygen to breathe. Over two hundred deaths have occurred among those climbing Mount Everest. One climber reached the top of Mount Everest, but, because of the deaths of fellow climbers, the victory was empty.

Among my five teammates who reached the top, four **perished** [died] *in a storm that blew in without warning while we were still high on the peak.*

—Jon Krakauer, *Into Thin Air: A Personal Account of the Mount Everest Disaster*

Directions: Sculpt the ordinary sentences into a paragraph *with four sentences.*

Sculpt the following information into the first sentence of your paragraph.

1a. I was straddling the top of the world.

1b. I had one foot in China and the other in Nepal.

1c. I cleared the ice from my oxygen mask.

1d. I hunched a shoulder against the wind.

1e. And I stared **absently** [*inattentively*] down at the vastness of Tibet.

Sculpt the following information into the second sentence of your paragraph.

2a. I understood something.

2b. It was about the sweep of earth beneath my feet.

2c. It was a spectacular sight.

Sculpt the following information into the <u>third sentence</u> of your paragraph.

3a. I had **fantasized** [*imagined*] about this moment.

3b. I had also fantasized about the release of emotion that would accompany this moment.

3c. I had had these fantasies for many months.

Sculpt the following information into the <u>fourth sentence</u> of your paragraph.

4a. Something happened now that I was finally here.

4b. It happened while I was actually standing on the summit of Mount Everest.

4c. What happened was that I didn't care.

Jon Krakauer, *Into Thin Air:*
A Personal Account of the Mount Everest Disaster (adapted)

ACTIVITY 7: EIFFEL TOWER

One of the most iconic structures in the world, the Eiffel Tower, as high as an eighty-story building, was built in Paris as the entranceway to the 1899 World's Fair held there. Since then, it has been visited by over 300 million people. A bold architectural feat, the Eiffel Tower was at the time of its construction the tallest man-made structure in the world.

With its Eiffel Tower, France did everything it could to
__ensure__ [guarantee] that its glory overwhelmed everyone.

—Erik Larson, *The Devil in the White City*

Directions: Sculpt the ordinary sentences into a paragraph *with six sentences*.

Sculpt the following information into the first sentence of your paragraph.

1a. The French did something that startled everyone.

1b. This happened in 1889.

Sculpt the following information into the second sentence of your paragraph.

2a. France opened a world's fair.

2b. The fair was in Paris.

2c. It was big and glamorous and exotic.

Sculpt the following information into the third sentence of your paragraph.

3a. At the heart of the fair stood a tower of iron.

3b. It rose one thousand feet into the sky.

3c. It was higher by far than any man-made structure on earth.

Sculpt the following information into the fourth sentence of your paragraph.

4a. The tower ensured the eternal fame of its designer.

4b. Its designer was Alexandre Gustave Eiffel.

Sculpt the following information into the fifth sentence of your paragraph.

5a. Eiffel's tower was forecast by Americans to be a monstrosity

5b. It would be a monstrosity that would **disfigure** [*scar*] forever the landscape of Paris.

5c. The tower turned out to possess unexpected style.

5d. Its style was with a sweeping base and **tapered** [*thinner*] shaft.

5e. Its shaft resembled the trail of a skyrocket.

Sculpt the following information into the <u>sixth sentence</u> of your paragraph.

6a. The tower was more than merely tall.

6b. The tower was grace.

6c. Its grace was frozen in iron.

Erik Larson, *The Devil in the White City* (adapted)

ACTIVITY 8: DISNEYLAND

Famous for widespread success as an amusement park, attracting guests from all over the world, Disneyland has over three thousand employees who speak at least one language in addition to English—over thirty different languages in all. On their name tags, multilingual employees include the languages they speak. Walt Disney and his family actually lived in Disneyland while the amusement park was being built.

Since its opening in 1955, more than 500 million people have visited The Happiest Place on Earth.

—Dinah Williams, *Secrets of Disneyland*

Directions: Sculpt the ordinary sentences into a paragraph *with six sentences*.

Sculpt the following information into the <u>first sentence</u> of your paragraph.

1a. The Disney family lived in Disneyland for a while.

1b. They lived there while Disneyland was being built.

1c. Walt Disney had an apartment created there for his family.

Sculpt the following information into the second sentence of your paragraph.

2a. There was a fire station there.

2b. The Disney apartment was built over the fire station.

2c. The apartment was on Main Street U.S.A. in Disneyland.

Sculpt the following information into the third sentence of your paragraph.

3a. Walt Disney did something while he was in that apartment.

3b. He would leave a light on.

3c. That light was burning in a window of the apartment.

Sculpt the following information into the fourth sentence of your paragraph.

4a. Disney died in 1966.

4b. Since then, something was done in his memory.

4d. What was done was leaving a light on.

4e. The light was in the window of the Disney apartment over the fire station.

Sculpt the following information into the fifth sentence of your paragraph.

5a. A fireman's pole led to the Disney apartment.

5b. It connected that apartment to the firehouse below the apartment.

Sculpt the following information into the sixth sentence of your paragraph.

6a. After something happened the top of the pole was sealed.

6b. What happened was that a guest climbed up the pole

6c. The guest climbed up to meet the Disney family.

Dinah Williams, *Secrets of Disneyland* (adapted)

ACTIVITY 9: EASTER ISLAND

On this Polynesian island, 887 ancient gigantic hand-carved stone statues have fascinated observers for centuries. The mystery of Easter Island's statues is based upon their size and weight and origin.

*The mystery surrounds how so few people on a **remote** [distant], treeless, and **impoverished** [poor] island could have made and transported hundreds of **eerie** [creepy] **gargantuan** [huge] statues for which the island is so famous.*

—Terry Hunt and Carol Lipo, *The Statues That Walked*

Directions: Sculpt the ordinary sentences into a paragraph *with five sentences*.

Sculpt the following information into the <u>first sentence</u> of your paragraph.

1a. Some stone statues stand nearly forty feet high.

1b. Some weigh more than seventy-five tons.

1c. They were carved out of the island's **quarry** [*pit*] of volcanic ash.

Sculpt the following information into the <u>second sentence</u> of your paragraph.

2a. They were then somehow transported several miles.

2b. They were transported over the island's **terrain** [*land*].

2c. The terrain was **rugged** [*uneven*].

Sculpt the following information into the <u>third sentence</u> of your paragraph.

3a. Many statues lie scattered across the island.

3b. They were never to take their **intended** [*planned*] places.

3c. Their intended places were on platforms.

3d. The platforms were along the shoreline.

Sculpt the following information into the <u>fourth sentence</u> of your paragraph.

4a. Many are situated on platforms.

4b. Those platforms are equally impressive.

Sculpt the following information into the <u>fifth sentence</u> of your paragraph.

5a. The statues are religious images.

5b. They face inward rather than out to sea.

5c. They seem to watch over their descendents.

5d. They watch day after day.

(adapted from Terry Hunt and Carol Lipo, *The Statues That Walked*)

ACTIVITY 10: ENDLESS CITY

Among the proposals from urban architects for skyscrapers of the future is this award-winning design, a city within a building, resembling a stack of pancakes soaring into London's sky. The proposed futuristic mixed-use skyscraper is a complete self-contained environment designed for housing future urban populations.

----

*As a remarkable building housing thousands of people
as well as shops and parks is **unveiled** [revealed], is the
Endless City what our horizons will look like one day?*

—Dominic Midgley, "Endless City: London's Skyline
of the Future Has Arrived Early," *Express*

Directions: Sculpt the ordinary sentences into a paragraph *with seven
sentences.*

**Sculpt the following information into the first sentence of your
paragraph.**

1a. The proposed future city is **christened** [*named*] Endless City.

1b. The proposed skyscraper is designed to soar a quarter of a mile.

1c. It will make it London's tallest building.

**Sculpt the following information into the second sentence of your
paragraph.**

2a. Something marks it out from its cloud-piercing peers, however.

2b. It is not size but facts about the inhabitants.

2c. Those inhabitants of the project will be able to work without leaving the
building.

2d. They will be able to rest without leaving the building.

2e. And they will be able to play without leaving the building.

**Sculpt the following information into the third sentence of your
paragraph.**

3a. It will be a mixed-use tower.

3b. It will house shops, offices, and entertainment **venues** [*places*] as well as
apartments.

3c. All of them will be linked by a series of ramps and walkways.

3d. The ramps and walkways will be around a hollow inner core.

Sculpt the following information into the <u>fourth sentence</u> of your paragraph.

4a. There will be thousands of residents in this vertical city.

4b. They will also be able to stroll in its streets, plazas, and huge parks.

4c. And those residents will be able to admire the surrounding cityscape from viewing platforms.

Sculpt the following information into the <u>fifth sentence</u> of your paragraph.

5a. Projects of this sort will be increasingly common.

5b. They will be common as the global race to the cities continues.

Sculpt the following information into the <u>sixth sentence</u> of your paragraph.

6a. Something will happen by 2050.

6b. What will happen is that three quarters of the world's population will live in cities.

Sculpt the following information into the <u>seventh sentence</u> of your paragraph.

7a. Urbanization and population growth is proceeding.

7b. They are proceeding at such a pace that the world will add one new city of a million people every five days.

7c. That will happen between now and 2050.

Dominic Midgley, "Endless City: London's Skyline
of the Future Has Arrived Early," *Express* (adapted)

YOUR TURN: RESEARCHED PARAGRAPH

Without imitating an author's paragraph but writing a paragraph so good it could have been by an author, research then write about a new remarkable place.

Directions: Select one of these remarkable places below. Choose one you haven't done earlier.

- -

1. Times Square, New York City, United States—*neon, flashy hub of the city*

2. Lotte World, Seoul, Korea—*world's largest indoor theme park*

3. Louvre Museum, Paris, France—*most visited museum in the world*

4. Forbidden City, Beijing, China—*home to many Chinese emperors*

5. Disney World, Orlando, Florida, United States—*amusement park with the Magic Kingdom*

6. Ocean Park, Hong Kong, China—*home of Hong Kong's biggest roller coaster, plus a huge maritime mammal park*

7. Sydney Opera House, Sydney, Australia—*group of linked buildings housing one of the world's largest and busiest arts centers*

8. Zocalo, Mexico City, Mexico—*area of one of the largest main squares and gathering places in the world*

9. Central Park, New York City, United States—*green oasis in the heart of the city featuring sports and entertainment events*

10. Grand Bazaar, Istanbul, Turkey—*immense outdoor market selling varied special products within fifteenth-century vaulted walkways*

11. Glacier Skywalk, Jasper National Park, Canadian Rockies, Canada—*thrilling glass walkway 918 feet above the ground for an unobstructed view downward*

12. One World Trade Center, New York City, United States—*replacement for the buildings destroyed in a terrorist attack and tallest building in Western Hemisphere*

13. Cinecitta World, Rome, Italy—*first theme park in the eternal city, featuring movie-related attractions and rides*

14. National Air and Space Museum, Washington, D.C., United States—*largest collection of aircraft and spacecraft in the world*

15. Tate Museum, London, United Kingdom—*world's most popular and largest collection of modern art*

16. Lincoln Memorial, Washington, D.C., United States—*monument honoring the sixteenth president of the United States*

17. Everland, Gyeonggi-Do, South Korea—*home to the world's steepest wooden roller coaster, plus a zoo and a water park*

18. Victoria Peak, Hong Kong, China—*highest mountain in Hong Kong with breathtaking views of the city*

19. Great Pyramid, El Giza, Egypt—*last one of the seven wonders of the ancient world still standing*

20. Taj Mahal, Agra, India—*jewel of Muslim art in India and regarded as one of the worlds' architectural masterpieces*

21. Nazca Desert, Peru—*site of enormous ancient drawings of mysterious origin on land*

22. Ice Hotel, Jukkasjarvi, Sweden—*hotel constructed of ice and snow and rebuilt each year*

23. Leap Castle, Roscrea, Ireland—*reportedly the most haunted castle in the world*

24. Varosha, Famagusta, Cyprus—*completely uninhabited abandoned resort town on the coast of Cyprus*

25. Mont St. Michel, Normandy, France—*famous landmark island protected during high tide from attacking armies*

- -

1. Learn more online or offline about the place you selected, and then draft and revise a paragraph about that place.

2. Pretend you are a writer for a print or online magazine that regularly features compellingly interesting information about remarkable places. Your job is to write an interesting informational paragraph about your chosen remarkable place.

3 Compose a paragraph that readers will believe was written by an author. Use a variety of sentence-composing tools in various positions: *openers*, *S-V splits*, *closers*.

4. Exchange your draft with other students in your class for suggestions to improve your paragraph, and give them suggestions, too. Then revise several times until your paragraph is finished.

5. Create a memorable title that your readers won't understand until after they read your paragraph. *Example:* "The Mysterious Moving Statues," a title for a paragraph about the gigantic ancient statues on Easter Island. No one knows how they moved many miles to the shoreline of the ocean.

REMARKABLE WORDS: FIGURATIVE LANGUAGE

Yelling to a rowdy crowd to get their attention in Shakespeare's play *Julius Caesar*, Mark Antony shouts, "Friends, Romans, Countrymen, lend me your ears!" Is he asking to borrow their ears, or for them to listen to him?

There are two kinds of meaning in the English language: literal and figurative. If something is meant literally, it means exactly what it says. If Mark Antony were speaking literally, he was in fact requesting the crowd to slice off their ears and give them to him. Of course, that meaning is absurd. He intends a figurative meaning. If something is meant figuratively, it means that some kind of comparison is intended. In Marc Antony's case, it is comparing ears to listening—since ears are the body part that listens.

Here's a simple example of figurative meaning, which is the language of comparison. "The snow was a white blanket." Literally snow isn't a blanket—white or otherwise. It's just snow. However, in the language of comparison snow can be compared to a white blanket because both share the same color and appearance. So, figuratively speaking, snow can be called a white blanket.

In figurative meaning, *A* equals *B*. *A* (the snow) equals *B* (a white blanket).

Get ready to study some remarkable words—figurative language, remarkable because it is often highly creative and memorable—and saturates our world in nonfiction and fiction, songs and poetry, advertising and slang, adding spice to the English language.

Understanding figurative language is a skill essential to understanding much of nonfiction and other kinds of writing, a skill practiced by effective readers and writers in and beyond middle school.

Friends, students, and scholars, please lend us your brains.

ACTIVITY 1: CONTRASTING LITERAL AND FIGURATIVE MEANING

In each pair, tell which meaning is figurative. Then explain what two things are being compared so that *A* equals *B*.

EXAMPLE

a. Time is valuable.

b. Time is money.

Explanation

In the first one, *A* equals *B* literally because time is something that shouldn't be wasted but used wisely.

In the second one, time is compared to money, so *A* equals *B* figuratively because both time and money are valuable and should be spent wisely.

1a. Life is a roller coaster.

1b. Life is a mix of good and bad times.

2a. America has a mix of different kinds of people that get along with each other.

2b. America is a melting pot.

3a. My computer is a dinosaur.

3b. My computer is **obsolete** [*outdated*].

4a. The highway at 5 P.M. was a parking lot.

4b. The traffic at 5 P.M. was at a standstill.

5a. Necessity is the mother of invention.

5b. A need inspires a solution.

    Figurative language adds spice to meaning, helping readers savor it. In that last sentence, what two "tasty" words are figurative?

ACTIVITY 2: ADDING FIGURATIVE LANGUAGE

Match the sentences in the left column to the figurative language in the right column. Then jot down the meaning of the sentence.

Sentences	Figurative Sentence Parts
1. Each snowflake is different, ^ , irreplaceable and beautiful. Julia Alvarez, "Snow"	**a.** like a captive on furlough **b.** as dead as a stone **c.** black mirrors a moment ago **d.** like a person **e.** **fluid** [*flowing*] black shadows
2. The first gray light had just appeared in the living room windows, ^ , now opening on the view of the woods to the south. Tracy Kidder, *Old Friends*	
3. Ahead of me, the chimpanzees, ^ , moved effortlessly. Jane Goodall, *Through a Window*	

4. ^ , Nazila wanted to store as much joy as fast as she could.
      Roya Hakakian,
      Journey from the Land of No	

5. The hanged prisoner was dangling with his toes pointed straight downward, **revolving** [*turning*] very slowly, ^ . George Orwell, "A Hanging"	

ACTIVITY 3: EXPLAINING FIGURATIVE IMAGES

Each quotation below conveys meaning through figurative language—the language of comparison. Explain the figurative language in the quotation, and then summarize the quotation *without using figurative language.*

EXAMPLE

Quotation: "Many people will walk in and out of your life, but only true friends will leave footprints in your heart."
Eleanor Roosevelt

Explanation of Figurative Language: The two figurative words are "walk" and "footprints." The quotation comments on the difference between acquaintances and friends. It suggests that we have many acquaintances whose lives interact with us, who "walk in and out of your life," but only special people become our friends because they matter deeply to us, leaving "footprints" in our hearts, that is, permanent value in our lives.

SAMPLE SUMMARIES OF THE QUOTATION

1. People come and go, but friends remain.

2. Only friends, not others, leave lasting impressions on our lives.

3. Those who matter to us deeply are true friends.

---

1. Every time you smile at someone, it is a gift to that person, a beautiful thing.

Mother Teresa

2. Friendship is like money, easier made than kept.

Samuel Barber

3. To the world you may be just one person, but to one person you may be the world.

Brandi Snyder

4. An investment in knowledge pays the best interest.

Benjamin Franklin

5. Technology brings you great gifts with one hand, and stabs you in the back with the other.

Carrie P. Snow

6. He who opens a school door closes a prison.

Victor Hugo

7. Love is a better teacher than duty.

Albert Einstein

8. Sports is a war without the killing.

Ted Turner

9. The higher we soar, the smaller we appear to those who cannot fly.

Friedrich Nietzsche

10. Fame is a vapor, popularity an accident, and riches take wings. Only one thing endures, and that is character.

Horace Greely

ACTIVITY 4: INTERPRETING FIGURATIVE IMAGES

Following is an excerpt from Diane Ackerman's book about how the brain works with a person's immune system to ward off sickness or disease. Figurative images are underlined. For each image, write a brief paragraph explaining what two things are being compared.

On the Mark: When you copy the words of the figurative image, enclose those words within quotation marks to show that they are Diane Ackerman's words, not yours.

EXAMPLE

In the second sentence, the phrase "merciless allies" refers to two things within the human body: the brain and the immune system. Those two parts work together in the way that allies in a war work together for the same goals, acting in a "merciless" manner because they together fight fearlessly and strongly to defeat the enemy, namely sickness or disease attacking the body.

(1) Is the brain part of the **immune** [*protection*] system, or is the immune system part of the brain? (2) They're in **cahoots** [*cooperation*], merciless allies, and they rarely forget a face. (3) Immune systems carry a grudge. (4) When special immune system cells find bacteria, fungi, viruses, or other invaders, they collect them and take them to one of the thousands of lymph nodes scattered around the body. (5) There T-helper cells receive the cargo and order B cells to manufacture antibodies, proteins that stick to the invaders and kill them. (6) Other immune cells save pieces of the invaders as memory aids. (7) They keep mumbling about the invader, and the next time it appears, the mumbling surges to an all-out war cry. (8) Only this time the immune system fights harder. (9) Our lymph nodes keep a roll call of each enemy—every flu and cold that **clobbered** [*attacked*]

us, last summer's pneumonia, the jellyfish stings in the Bahamas, the chicken pox and measles, the protozoan imbibed while snorkeling in the Amazon, and all the inoculations, too. (10) <u>An internal police state</u>, the immune system **monitors** [*watches*] known <u>troublemakers</u>, and to be safe, <u>all strangers in general.</u>

Because we do not understand the brain very well we are constantly tempted to use the latest technology as a model for trying to understand it. In my childhood we were always assured that the brain was a telephone switchboard. ("What else could it be?") Sherrington, the great British neuroscientist, thought that the brain worked like a telegraph system. Freud often compared the brain to hydraulic and electro-magnetic systems. Leibniz compared it to a mill, and I am told some of the ancient Greeks thought the brain functions like a catapult. At present, obviously, the metaphor is the digital computer.

—John R. Searle, *Minds, Brains, and Science*

ACTIVITY 5: KINDS OF FIGURATIVE LANGUAGE

There are two main kinds of language of comparison: metaphor and simile.

A metaphor compares *A* to *B*.

METAPHOR: "Jealousy is the grave of affection."

Mary Baker Eddy

A simile compares *A* to *B* directly through the use of the words *like* or *as*.

> SIMILE: "Jealousy is like a hot pepper. Use it mildly, and you add spice to the relationship. Use too much of it and it can burn."

> Ayala M. Pines

In each quotation below, *A* is compared to *B*, either through a metaphor or a simile.

Directions: For each, complete this equation: *A* equals *B* because . . .

EXAMPLE

> *Quotation:* "Ahead of me, the chimpanzees, fluid black shadows, moved effortlessly."
> Jane Goodall, *Through a Window*

> *Explanation of Figurative Language:* "Chimpanzees" (*A*) equal "fluid black shadows" (*B*) because of their smooth movements and their dark color.

On the Mark: When you copy the figurative wording, enclose those words within quotation marks to show that they are the author's words, not yours.

METAPHORS

1. Goodness is the only investment that never fails.

   Henry David Thoreau

2. Failure is the condiment that gives success its flavor.

   Truman Capote

3. Laughter is a tranquilizer with no side effects.

   Arnold H. Glasgow

4. The self is merely the lens through which we see others and the world.

Anaïs Nin

5. Mr. Hunt was a frown in a suit, with a client list that included most of America's richest families.

Erik Larson, *The Devil in the White City*

SIMILES

6. Life is like a box of chocolates because you never know what you're gonna get.

Winston Groom, *Forrest Gump*

7. The mist hung in the air like a prancing unicorn.

Graham Joyce, *The Silent Land*

8. Justice is like a train that's nearly always late.

Yevgeny Yevtushenko

9. A two-year-old is like having a blender, but you don't have a top for it.

Jerry Seinfeld

10. The word carpentry is like any other kind of carpentry because you must join your sentences smoothly.

Anatole France

ACTIVITY 6: DEFINING METAPHOR

Metaphor, the most common kind of figurative language, compares two different things through a connection between them. Each quotation below conveys some aspect of metaphor. In one paragraph, choose *one* quotation and explain it so thoroughly and clearly that your explanation is understandable to other students.

EXAMPLE

Quotation: "Metaphors have a way of holding the most truth in the least space."

Orson Scott Card, author of *Ender's Game*

Explanation

A metaphor is an invisible comparison of two things. For example, if you say, "The fierce wind was a monster," you are comparing wind to a monster. That sentence has just six words, but says a lot. The details are invisible but people know that both fierce wind and a monster are threatening, make loud noises, cause fear, and so forth. The comparison of fierce wind to a monster is condensed. A metaphor condenses a comparison.

----

1. Sports is a metaphor for overcoming obstacles and achieving against great odds.

   Bill Bradley

2. A garden is a metaphor for life.

   Larry Dossey

3. Bridges are a metaphor for everything in life.

   Jim West

4. Families are a metaphor for every other part of society.

   Anna Quindlen

5. A metaphor is the skeleton key to unlock the mind of any student.

   Grant Fairley

6. Life, as the most ancient of all metaphors insists, is a journey.

    Jonathan Raban

7. You can't think without metaphors.

    Mary Catherine Bateson

8. Surfing is a kind of good metaphor for life.

    Jaimal Yogis

9. The metaphor of the melting pot for the United States is unfortunate and misleading. A more accurate metaphor would be a salad bowl, for, though salad is an **entity** [*one object*], the lettuce can still be **distinguished** [*told apart*] from the chicory, the tomatoes from the cabbage.

    Carl N. Degler

10. Together a brick and a blanket create the perfect metaphor for life. Will you be a brick and make something of your life, or be a blanket and sleep your life away?

    Amy Summers

To be a master of metaphor . . . is a sign of genius, since a good metaphor implies an intuitive perception of the similarities in dissimilarities.

—Aristotle

YOUR TURN: EXPLANATORY PARAGRAPH

Choose one of the figurative quotations below. Write a paragraph that has three purposes:

- to explain the figurative meaning

- to give a detailed example of the quotation from someone's life or your imagination

- to include examples of each of these sentence-composing tools: openers, S-V splits, closers.

EXAMPLE

Figurative Quotation

If a man does not keep pace with his companions, perhaps it is because he hears a different drummer. Let him step to the music which he hears, however measured or far away.

Henry David Thoreau

Sample Paragraph: The writer, fascinated with modern art, knows that artist Salvador Dali was a nonconformist who did "not keep pace with his companions." The writer researched Dali's life, and then wrote this paragraph.

(1) If a man does not act like the people around him, it might be because he has different thoughts and feelings that cause him to see things in a new way. (2) Let him do what he is comfortable doing, even if it seems very different from everyone else. (3) A pioneer in modern art, an original thinker, Salvador Dali painted surrealistic images, not mirroring reality, because he saw his subjects in both sculpture and painting with originality. (4) In addition to his nonconforming artworks, Dali, always wearing a long pencil-thin mustache almost touching his eyebrows, led an eccentric life, attracting critics and fans with his bizarre clothing and flamboyant behavior. (5) Dali, outrageous and fascinating, always surprised his public.

SENTENCE-COMPOSING TOOLS

The writer uses all three positions. The skillful use of the tools adds interesting descriptive details and strong sentence structure. As a result, the paragraph resembles the way an author writes.

OPENERS:
(To review these, please see pages 48–54.)

- If a man does not act like the people around him
- A pioneer in modern art, an original thinker
- In addition to his nonconforming artworks

S-V SPLITS:
(To review these, please see pages 55–61.)

- always wearing a long pencil-thin mustache almost touching his eyebrows
- outrageous and fascinating

CLOSERS:
(To review these, please see pages 62–68.)

- even if it seems very different from everyone else
- not mirroring reality
- because he saw his subjects in both sculpture and painting with originality
- attracting critics and fans with his bizarre clothing and flamboyant behavior

FIGURATIVE QUOTATIONS (*Choose one.*)

1. There are two ways of spreading light: to be the candle, or the mirror that reflects it.

   Edith Wharton

2. Life is like riding a bicycle. To keep your balance you must keep moving.

   Albert Einstein

3. Courage is the ladder on which all the other virtues mount.

   Clare Booth Luce

4. In the book of life, the answers aren't in the back.

   Charles M. Schulz

5. Fame is a pearl many dive for and only a few bring up.

   Louisa May Alcott

6. Procrastination is the thief of time.

   Edward Young

7. Everyone is a moon, and has a dark side which he or she never shows to anybody.

   Mark Twain

8. The human mind treats a new idea the same way the body treats a strange protein. It rejects it.

   Peter B. Medawar

9. The scenes of our life are like pictures done in rough mosaic. Looked at close-up they produce no effect. There is nothing beautiful to be found in them, unless you stand some distance off.

   Arthur Schopenhauer

10. No man is an island entire of itself. Every man is a piece of the continent, a part of the main; if a clod be washed away by the sea, Europe is the less. Any man's death diminishes me, because I am involved in mankind. Therefore, never send to know for whom the bell tolls; it tolls for thee.

    John Donne (adapted)

REMARKABLE STATEMENTS: QUOTABLE QUOTES

An essay is a common type of nonfiction, a short expression of an author's knowledge or opinion about a topic.

The essay is a literary device for saying almost anything about almost anything.

—Aldous Huxley

Essays communicate authoritative or compelling opinions about a topic, carefully worded and structured. What a good essay says is memorable for some reason: because it's witty, profound, insightful, wise, authoritative, or some other quality that makes it worth reading and remembering.

Essays can be various lengths. In this section, you'll study bite-size essays—short quotations—that say "almost anything about almost everything."

Bite-size essays, often called *famous quotes* or *pearls of wisdom*, express an opinion about a topic, rendered memorably, sometimes reflecting a common idea but uncommonly expressed.

Some essays are to be tasted, others swallowed, and some few chewed and digested.

—Francis Bacon

Just as you need physical food for physical strength, you need intellectual food for intellectual strength. In this section, you'll feed on intellectual food—quotable quotes—to nourish your mind. You'll decide which quotations should be merely tasted, which absolutely swallowed, and which thoroughly chewed and digested. Many are truly delicious.

ACTIVITY 1: CHUNKING BITE-SIZE ESSAYS

To savor these little essays, take a bite at a time by chunking them. The chunked quotations below are all about the same topic: FRIENDSHIP.

A good chunk makes sense by itself; it "tastes" good. A bad chunk doesn't make sense by itself; it "tastes" bad.

Read each chunk to the slash mark (/) and you'll be able to see the difference between bad chunks (*left column*) and good chunks (*right column*). To read well, chunk well, and then take a bite of the essay to see how it tastes. Chunking improves your ability to read with understanding.

Bad Chunks	Good Chunks
1a. A true / friend is one soul in two / bodies.	**1b.** A true friend / is one soul / in two bodies. Aristotle
2a. Friendship improves happiness, lessens / misery, by doubling our / joys, and dividing our / grief.	**2b.** Friendship improves happiness, / lessens misery, / by doubling our joys, / and dividing our grief. Joseph Addison
3a. Friendship is the only / cement that will / ever hold the / world together.	**3b.** Friendship / is the only cement / that will ever / hold the world together. Woodrow Wilson
4a. If you go looking for a / friend, you're going to find that they are very / scarce, but if you go / out to be a / friend, you'll find them everywhere.	**4b.** If you go looking for a friend, / you're going to find / that they are very scarce, / but if you go out to be a friend, / you'll find them everywhere. Zig Ziglar

ACTIVITY 2: FINDING CHUNKS

Read each pair of sentences a chunk at a time. Tell which has good chunks, and which has bad chunks. <u>Important</u>: Read out loud, and pause where each slash mark (/) occurs. If it doesn't make sense, the chunks are bad. If it makes sense, the chunks are good.

EXAMPLE

    a. If at first you don't / succeed then skydiving definitely isn't for / you.

    b. If at first you don't succeed / then skydiving / definitely isn't for you.

Steven Wright

GOOD CHUNKS: **b**

1a. You cannot / fly like an eagle / with wings of a wren.

1b. You cannot fly like / an eagle with wings / of a wren.

William Henry Hudson

2a. Happiness adds and / multiples, as we divide / it with others.

2b. Happiness adds and multiples, / as we divide it / with others.

Waldemar A. Nielson

3a. The person who does not read books / has no advantage / over the person / who can not read them.

3b. The person who does / not read books has no / advantage over the person who can / not read them.

Mark Twain

4a. Nothing is / impossible because the / word itself / says, "I'm possible!"

4b. Nothing / is impossible / because the word itself / says, "I'm possible!"

Audrey Hepburn

5a. Try to / be a / rainbow in someone's / cloud.

5b. Try / to be / a rainbow / in someone's cloud.

Maya Angelou

6a. There is no / cosmetic for / beauty like / happiness.

6b. There is / no cosmetic / for beauty / like happiness.

Maria Mitchell

7a. Try to learn something / about everything / and everything / about something.

7b. Try to / learn something about / everything and everything about / something.

Thomas Huxley

8a. The great thing / about getting older / is that you don't lose / all the other ages you've been.

8b. The great thing about getting / older is that you don't / lose all the other ages you've / been.

Madeleine L'Engle

9a. Like a welcome summer rain, / humor may suddenly / cleanse and clear the earth, / the air, and you.

9b. Like a / welcome summer rain, humor may suddenly / cleanse and clear the earth, the / air, and you.

Langston Hughes

10a. Friendships in / childhood are usually a / matter of chance, whereas in adolescence they are most / often a matter of / choice.

10b. Friendships in childhood / are usually a matter of chance, / whereas in adolescence / they are most often / a matter of choice.

David Elkind

ACTIVITY 3: MARKING GOOD CHUNKS

Quotations below are chunked meaninglessly. Copy each, and using the same number of slash marks, chunk the quotation meaningfully.

EXAMPLE

Meaningless Chunks
To know what / is right and not / do it is / the worst cowardice.

Meaningful Chunks
To know /what is right / and not do it / is the worst cowardice.

Confucius

---

1. A penny / saved is a penny earned.

    Benjamin Franklin

2. Friendship is like / money, easier made than / kept.

    Samuel Butler

3. Any sufficiently advanced / technology is **indistinguishable** [*not different*] from / magic.

    Arthur C. Clark

4. Your **attitude** [*outlook*], not your / **aptitude** [*ability*], will determine your / **altitude** [*height*].

    Zig Ziglar

5. If you do / not think about your future, you cannot / have one.

    John Galsworthy

6. It is health that / is real / wealth, not pieces of / gold and silver.

Mahatma Gandhi

7. When you are content to / be simply / yourself and don't compare or compete, everybody will respect / you.

Lao Tzu

8. Do not / go where the path may / lead but instead go where there is no / path and / leave a trail.

Ralph Waldo Emerson

9. Anger is an / acid that can / do more harm to the / **vessel** [*container*] in which it is / stored than to anything on which it is / poured.

Mark Twain

10. The practice of patience toward / one another, the overlooking of one another's / **defects** [*faults*], and the **bearing** [*carrying*] of one / another's **burdens** [*hardships*] is the most **elementary** [*basic*] condition of all human and social activity in the / family, and in / society.

Lawrence G. Lovasik

ACTIVITY 4: MATCHING QUOTATIONS WITH MEANINGS

Match the quotation in the left column with its meaning in the right column.

Quotation: Part One (1–5)	Meaning
1. Adolescence is a new birth, for the higher and more completely human traits are now born. G. Stanley Hall	**a.** Time is fast when you are having a good time.
2. The true sign of intelligence is not knowledge but imagination. Albert Einstein	**b.** Sometimes you win second prize, not first, but it's better than no prize. **c.** A person gains maturity after childhood.
3. All our sweetest hours fly fastest. Virgil	**d.** The future often contains unexpected joy.
4. If you aim for the moon and miss, you may hit a star. W. Clement Stone	**e.** Really smart people think creatively.
5. Our brightest blazes of gladness are commonly kindled by unexpected sparks.	

Quotation: Part Two (6–10)	Meaning: Part Two
6. Mistakes are the portals [doorways] of discovery. James Joyce	**f.** Optimism cancels pessimism. **g.** If you want something to occur, make it happen.
7. Rough diamonds may sometimes be mistaken for worthless pebbles. Thomas Browne	**h.** Sometimes valuable things at first seem worthless. **i.** For contentment, give more than you get.
8. The best way to predict the future is to create it. Peter Drucker	**j.** Mistakes can yield new ideas.
9. Keep your face to the sunshine and you cannot see a shadow. Helen Keller	
10. Remember that the happiest persons aren't those getting more but those giving more. H. Jackson Brown, Jr.	

ACTIVITY 5: IDENTIFYING GOOD PARAPHRASES

A paraphrase is a rewrite of a quotation, keeping the same meaning but changing most of the words. Choose the statement that is the better paraphrase of the quotation.

EXAMPLE

Quotation: The only thing more expensive than education is ignorance.

Benjamin Franklin

a. *weak paraphrase*—Ignorance causes people to regret getting an education.

b. *strong paraphrase*—Ignorance costs society problems that education could avoid.

Explanation: Choice **b** paraphrases the quotation. It clearly explains that the uneducated may cause social problems costly to solve.

---

1. Laughter is the sun that drives winter from the human face.

Victor Hugo

   a. The warmth of laughter changes an emotionless face.

   b. Laughing with someone helps them cheer up.

2. Seven days without laughter make one weak.

Anonymous

   a. Weakness results from seriousness.

   b. Frequent laughter creates emotional strength.

3. The human race has one really effective weapon, and that is laughter.

Mark Twain

   a. Laughing together can make enemies friends.

   b. Laughing at someone can be more horrible than a gunshot.

4. The most wasted of all days is one without laughter.

e. e. Cummings

   a. A good day is one with fun.

   b. A bad day is one without laughter.

5. The person who can bring the spirit of laughter into a room is indeed blessed.

—Bennett Cerf

   a. People are grateful to someone who laughs.

   b. A person who can inspire laughter in others is special.

Directions: The preceding five quotations are about laughter. In just one or two sentences, write your opinion about laughter, expressed, like those quotations, memorably.

TOPIC: SIBLINGS

6. A sister is a little bit of childhood that can never be lost.

Marian C. Gerretty

   a. When girls are sisters, they always seem very much like children.

   b. A sister helps you remember what it was like to be a child.

7. Comparison is a **death knell** [*destruction*] to sibling harmony.

Elizabeth Fishel

   a. To get along, siblings shouldn't compare themselves.

   b. Arguing between siblings is inevitable.

8. Either men will learn to live as brothers, or they will die like beasts.

Max Lerner

   a. Either men will learn to live as family, or they will die like animals.

   b. Either people will cooperate with each other, or they will harm each other.

9. **Repose** [*rest*] is a good thing, but boredom is its brother.

Voltaire

    a. Rest is refreshing, but can become boring if done too long.

    b. Boredom comes from not enough meaningful and varied activities.

10. I do not believe that the accident of birth makes people brothers and sisters. It makes them siblings. Sisterhood and brotherhood are conditions people have to work at.

Maya Angelou

    a. Nature creates siblings, but people create sisterhood and brotherhood.

    b. Being a good sibling, whether a brother or sister, takes hard work.

Directions: The preceding five quotations are about siblings. In just one or two sentences, write your opinion about siblings, expressed, like those quotations, memorably.

TOPIC: EDUCATION

11. To the uneducated, an A is just three sticks.

A. A. Milne

    a. The ignorant are illiterate.

    b. Readers understand the alphabet.

12. He who opens a school door closes a prison door.

Victor Hugo

    a. Prisons should provide education.

    b. Education helps prevent crime.

13. The progress of the world depends almost entirely on education.

George Eastman

   a. Most good things in the world are done by educated people.

   b. Most worldwide improvements result from education.

14. Give a man a fish and he eats for a day. Teach a man to fish and he eats for a lifetime.

Maimonides

   a. Providing something is not as valuable as teaching how to get it.

   b. Fishing is a skill that can provide food for a long time.

15. The whole purpose of education is to turn mirrors into windows.

Sydney J. Harris

   a. Education aims to reflect truths about learners.

   b. Education broadens the **perspective** [*understanding*] of learners.

Directions: The preceding five quotations are about education. In just one or two sentences, write your opinion about education, expressed, like those quotations, memorably.

TOPIC: TECHNOLOGY

16. Technology is a useful servant but a dangerous master.

Christian Lous Lange

   a. Technology should be used but not depended upon.

   b. Technology should not control people but serve them.

17. Every aspect of technology has a dark side, including the bow and arrow.

Margaret Atwood

a. All technology, including primitive weapons, presents problems.

b. Weapons, present and past, reflect the ugly side of technology.

18. Civilization advances by **extending** [*increasing*] the number of important operations we can perform without thinking about them.

Alfred North Whitehead

a. Humanity improves when people stop thinking about everything.

b. Progress through technology automates important procedures.

19. As our technological **powers** [*strengths*] increase, the side effects and potential hazards also **escalate** [*increase*].

Alvin Toffler

a. When technology advances, it may become more dangerous.

b. Technology can be harmful instead of helpful.

20. One machine can do the work of fifty **ordinary** [*common*] people. No machine can do the work of one **extraordinary** [*uncommon*] person.

Elbert Hubbard

a. A machine can do the work of many people, but not one person.

b. The work of a special unique person cannot be done by a machine.

Directions: The preceding five quotations are about technology. In just one or two sentences, write your opinion about technology, expressed, like those quotations, memorably.

ACTIVITY 6: PARAPHRASING QUOTATIONS

A paraphrase expresses equivalent meaning. For each quotation, write a paraphrase with a similar meaning as the quotation, but written mostly in your own words.

EXAMPLE

> *Quotation:* Fatigue is the best pillow.
>
> Benjamin Franklin

> *Meaning:* People sleep well after working hard.

> ***Sample Good Paraphrases***
>
> 1. A good sleep results from being really tired.
>
> 2. To sleep well, first work hard to tire yourself out.
>
> 3. Exhaustion often leads to great sleep.

-----

1. A friend in need is a friend indeed.

   Richard Graves

2. Winners never quit, and quitters never win.

   Vince Lombardi

3. A smile is happiness you'll find right under your nose.

   Tom Wilson

4. The trust of the innocent is the liar's most useful tool.

   Stephen King

5. The best place to find a helping hand is at the end of your own arm.

Swedish proverb

6. If you think you can, or if you think you can't, you're probably right.

Henry Ford

7. The only thing we have to fear is fear itself.

Franklin D. Roosevelt

8. When life gives you lemons, make lemonade.

Julius Rosenwald

9. No one can really pull you up very high because you lose your grip on the rope. On your own two feet, though, you can climb mountains.

Louis Brandeis

10. Nothing is a greater **impediment** [*obstacle*] to being on good terms with others than being **ill-at-ease** [*uncomfortable*] with yourself.

Honore de Balzac

ACTIVITY 7: TRANSLATING FIGURATIVE QUOTATIONS

Each quotation below expresses meaning through figurative language—the language of comparison. Translate each quotation *without using figurative language*. (You can review figurative language in the section "REMARKABLE WORDS: FIGURATIVE LANGUAGE" on pages 170–184.)

EXAMPLE

Figurative Quotation: There is no greater loan than a sympathetic ear.

Frank Tyger

Figurative Language: This quotation taken literally makes no sense because it's impossible to loan somebody your ear. The meaning, then, must be figurative, comparing a loan and an ear to other things. To *loan* is to give someone something of value, not permanently but temporarily. An *ear* is the organ of hearing. What is a "sympathetic" ear? To sympathize is to help someone during their difficulties.

Sample Translation: The best help for someone troubled is to listen.

----

1. Big sisters are the **crabgrass** [*weeds*] in the lawn of life.

    Charles M. Schulz

2. **Persistence** [*perseverance*] is the price of success.

    David DeAngelo

3. Those who trim themselves to suit everyone will soon **whittle** [*carve*] themselves away.

    Raymond Hull

4. Success **breeds** [*produces*] success.

    Mia Hamm

5. Those who think it is **permissible** [*okay*] to tell white lies soon grow color-blind.

    Austin O'Malley

6. A friend knows the song in my heart and sings it to me when my memory fails.

    Donna Roberts

7. **Mirth** [*laughter*] is God's medicine.

Henry Ward Beecher

8. Turn your wounds into wisdom.

Oprah Winfrey

9. A book is a gift you can open again and again.

Garrison Keiller

10. Genius without education is like silver in the mine.

Benjamin Franklin

YOUR TURN: TRUE STORY

Choose one of the quotations from anywhere in this section (*pages 185–201*) that illustrates something from your own life or the life of another person you know.

Directions:

1. Write a true story (a nonfictional narrative) two to three double-spaced pages long illustrating your chosen quotation.

2. To tell the story, use third-person pronouns, not first-person pronouns, even if you are writing a story about yourself.

FIRST-PERSON PRONOUNS: *I, me, my, mine*
I went to the doctor, a close friend of mine, who told me that my weight was a few pounds up from last time, reassuring me that the increase was nothing for me to worry about.

THIRD-PERSON PRONOUNS: *he/she, him/her, his/her, his/hers*
He went to the doctor, a close friend of his, who told him that his weight was a few pounds up from last time, reassuring him that the increase was nothing for him to worry about.

or

> She went to the doctor, a close friend of hers, who told her that her weight was a few pounds up from last time, reassuring her that the increase was nothing for her to worry about.

3. Don't visibly include your chosen quotation within your true story. Instead, invisibly illustrate it throughout the story. In other words, don't state the quotation but imply it.

4. Include varied examples of sentence-composing tools you learned earlier:

   OPENERS (*pages 48–54*)

   S-V SPLITS (*pages 55–61*)

   CLOSERS (*pages 62–68*)

See the following sample student paper, which includes all three tools.

5. Exchange your draft with peers for suggestions for improvement. Provide peers a list of three quotations from this section, one of which your story illustrates. See if peers can guess that quotation.

Below is a sample essay by a student named Danny about a baseball game he played as a young boy with his three cousins and their friends. Compared to them, Danny, whose strength was creativity not athletics, felt very inadequate as an athlete.

Danny wrote the story about himself, but used third-person not first-person pronouns—for example, *he* not *I*, *him* not *me*. As a result, it reads as if it's someone else's story. He began by first choosing one of the quotations from this section on pages 185–201 that the story would illustrate. From the three quotations below, tell which one Danny's story illustrates. Cite evidence supporting your claim by quoting from Danny's essay.

1. Comparison is a **death knell** [*destruction*] to sibling harmony.

   Elizabeth Fishel

2. If you think you can, or if you think you can't, you're probably right.

   Henry Ford

3. Those who trim themselves to suit everyone will soon **whittle** [*carve*] themselves away.

   Raymond Hull

"Life-Altering Force"
by Daniel Gunderson
(*a student paper*)

(1) One of the boys named Ronny Phillips, a pimply guy with a silver cross dangling from his neck on a chain, carried a baseball bat in a homemade sling on his back. (2) Head cast down, thumbs twiddling nervously as he awaited his turn at bat, Ronny, a timid loner, the youngest and smallest of the four cousins, found himself wishing that his aunt had just let him stay at the house. (3) Instead, she forced him to join his three older cousins and their athletic friends in a game of baseball, a sport requiring quick reflexes and agility beyond Ronny's capability. (4) Feeling like a rookie among champions, Ronny compared his physical attributes with those of his three cousins and their highly able-bodied friends, convinced he simply could not measure up.

(5) Matthew, the oldest of Ronny's cousins, had legs so strong that it seemed like he could jump up and catch a ball, no matter how high. (6) A ruthless pitcher, Royce, the middle cousin, could throw anything from a slow, underhanded floater to a fastball with enough force to knock the bat out of a player's hands. (7) Eddie, the youngest of the three, his legs the fastest things on the field other than his mouth, could run the whole way around the baseball diamond before the ball even hit ground. (8) Each brother possessed skills that provided him a significant advantage in baseball.

(9) Ronny, with no athletic abilities whatsoever, was not similarly skilled. (10) When Ronny reviewed his own talents, the only thing that came to mind was making comic books, an ability emphatically unrelated to skills required for baseball. (11) Typically and often, Ronny's free time would be spent in his room, his body outstretched on the floor and his mouth full of M&M's, writing about ordinary individuals who encountered some life-altering force which granted them extraordinary abilities. (12) That talent was purely intellectual. (13) For physical activity, he had an extremely low tolerance, plus a face full of bulging zits whereas his cousins had bulging muscles.

(14) Barely understanding the rules of baseball, the odds clearly against him, Ronny snapped out of his daydream when he was called to bat. (15) Standing at home plate, Ronny looked at the pitcher's mound and locked eyes with Royce, the breaker of batters, his mean smile striking fear into the heart of his next victim. (16) Hands shaking, Ronny slowly drew his bat from the sling on his back. (17) He just prayed it would be over quickly, wishing he could be blessed by some life-altering force like the characters he created in his home-made comic books.

(18) For ball one, Ronny swung and missed. (19) For ball two, he swung harder but missed. (20) For ball three, voices of his comic book characters in Ronny's imagination coaching and cheering, he swung and slammed the ball hard. (21) Up and higher up, the ball flew fast and even higher, as Ronny's heart soared.

THE IMPORTANCE OF SENTENCE-COMPOSING TOOLS

Two versions of Daniel's story are below, the first without sentence-composing tools, the second—Daniel's original version—with tools. Notice how much more information is in the original story by Daniel, conveyed through sentence-composing tools in a mix of positions: *opener, S-V split, closer*.

WITHOUT TOOLS (*115 words*)

(1) One of the boys named Ronny Phillips carried a baseball bat in a homemade sling on his back. (2) Ronny found himself wishing that his

aunt had just let him stay at the house. (3) She forced him to join his three older cousins and their athletic friends in a game of baseball. (4) Ronny compared his physical attributes with those of his three cousins and their highly able-bodied friends.

(5) Matthew had legs so strong that it seemed like he could jump up and catch a ball. (6) Royce could throw anything from a slow, underhanded floater to a fastball with enough force to knock the bat out of a player's hands. (7) Eddie could run the whole way around the baseball diamond before the ball even hit ground. (8) Each brother possessed skills that provided him a significant advantage in baseball.

(9) Ronny was not similarly skilled. (10) The only thing that came to mind was making comic books. (11) Ronny's free time would be spent in his room. (12) That talent was purely intellectual. (13) He had an extremely low tolerance.

(14) Ronny snapped out of his daydream when he was called to bat. (15) Ronny looked at the pitcher's mound and locked eyes with Royce. (16) Ronny slowly drew his bat from the sling on his back. (17) He just prayed it would be over quickly.

(18) Ronny swung and missed. (19) He swung harder but missed. (20) He swung and slammed the ball hard. (21) The ball flew fast and even higher.

TOOLS IN MIXED POSITIONS (Bolded)
478 words (*almost two-thirds tools*)

(1) One of the boys named Ronny Phillips, **a pimply guy with a silver cross dangling from his neck on a chain**, carried a baseball bat in a homemade sling on his back. (2) **Head cast down, thumbs twiddling nervously as he awaited his turn at bat**, Ronny, **a timid loner, the youngest and smallest of the four cousins**, found himself wishing that his aunt had just let him stay at the house. (3) **Instead**, she forced him to join his three older cousins and their athletic friends in a game of baseball, **a sport requiring quick reflexes and agility beyond**

Ronny's capability. (4) **Feeling like a rookie among champions,** Ronny compared his physical attributes with those of his three cousins and their highly able-bodied friends, **convinced he simply could not measure up**.

(5) Matthew, **the oldest of Ronny's cousins,** had legs so strong that it seemed like he could jump up and catch a ball, **no matter how high**. (6) **A ruthless pitcher,** Royce, **the middle cousin,** could throw anything from a slow, underhanded floater to a fastball with enough force to knock the bat out of a player's hands. (7) Eddie, **the youngest of the three, his legs the fastest things on the field other than his mouth,** could run the whole way around the baseball diamond before the ball even hit ground. (8) Each brother possessed skills that provided him a significant advantage in baseball.

(9) Ronny, **with no athletic abilities whatsoever,** was not similarly skilled. (10) **When Ronny reviewed his own talents,** the only thing that came to mind was making comic books, **an ability emphatically unrelated to skills required for baseball**. (11) **Typically and often,** Ronny's free time would be spent in his room, **his body outstretched on the floor and his mouth full of M&M's,** writing about ordinary individuals who encountered some life-altering force which granted them extraordinary abilities. (12) That talent was purely intellectual. (13) **For physical activity,** he had an extremely low tolerance, **plus a face full of bulging zits whereas his cousins had bulging muscles**.

(14) **Barely understanding the rules of baseball, the odds clearly against him,** Ronny snapped out of his daydream when he was called to bat. (15) **Standing at home plate,** Ronny looked at the pitcher's mound and locked eyes with Royce, **the breaker of batters, his mean smile striking fear into the heart of his next victim**. (16) **Hands shaking,** Ronny slowly drew his bat from the sling on his back. (17) He just prayed it would be over quickly, **wishing he could be blessed by some life-altering force like the characters he created in his home-made comic books**.

(18) **For ball one**, Ronny swung and missed. (19) **For ball two**, he swung harder but missed. (20) **For ball three, voices of his comic book characters in Ronny's imagination coaching and cheering**, he swung and slammed the ball hard. (21) **Up and higher up**, the ball flew fast and even higher, **as Ronny's heart soared**.

TOOLS BY POSITION

Important: Notice that each tool is a *sentence part*, not a complete sentence.

OPENERS (*tools at the beginning of a sentence*)

- head cast down
- thumbs twiddling nervously as he awaited his turn at bat
- instead
- feeling like a rookie among champions
- a ruthless pitcher
- when Ronny reviewed his own talents
- typically and often
- for physical activity
- barely understanding the rules of baseball
- the odds clearly against him
- standing at home plate
- hands shaking
- for ball one
- for ball two

- for ball three
- voices of his comic book characters in Ronny's imagination coaching and cheering
- up and higher up

S-V SPLITS (*tools between a subject and verb*)

- a pimply guy with a silver cross dangling from his neck on a chain
- a timid loner
- the youngest and smallest of the four cousins
- the oldest of Ronny's cousins
- the middle cousin
- the youngest of the three
- his legs the fastest things on the field other than his mouth
- with no athletic abilities whatsoever

CLOSERS (*tools at the end of a sentence*)

- a sport requiring quick reflexes and agility beyond Ronny's capability
- convinced he simply could not measure up
- no matter how high
- an ability emphatically unrelated to skills required for baseball
- his body outstretched on the floor and his mouth full of M&M's
- writing about ordinary individuals who encountered some life-altering force which granted them extraordinary abilities
- plus a face full of bulging zits whereas his cousins had bulging muscles
- the breaker of batters

- his mean smile striking fear into the heart of his next victim
- wishing he could be blessed by some life-altering force like the characters he created in his home-made comic books
- as Ronny's heart soared

Clearly, the version with sentence-composing tools is much stronger than the one without tools, providing more information, important details, and mature style. Using sentence-composing tools within your own sentences—*openers*, *S-V splits*, *closers*—strengthens your writing.

What's important is that you have faith in people, that they're basically good and smart, and if you give them tools, they'll do wonderful things with them.

—Steve Jobs

SENTENCE COMPOSING: TEACHING TO LEARN

Sometimes the best way to learn something is to teach it. In preparing to teach something, then teaching it, you must first learn what is to be taught. For your final activity of *Nonfiction for Middle School: A Sentence-Composing Approach*, you'll see how this works. Here, you'll deepen what you've already learned—by teaching it.

Imagine you have been hired by a textbook publisher to write activities to teach students how to build better sentences.

Here's how you do your job. Directions are below.

PART ONE: CHOOSING WHAT YOU'LL TEACH

Choose one of the three positions—*opener, S-V split, closer*—to teach how good writers use that position.

To begin preparing, first thoroughly review how those positions are taught earlier in this worktext:

- *openers* (pages 48–54)

- *S-V splits* (pages 55–61)

- *closers* (pages 62–68).

PART TWO: GATHERING YOUR MATERIALS OF INSTRUCTION

You need at least fifteen well-built nonfiction sentences for your lesson on the position you've chosen.

Following are examples of tools as *openers, S-V splits, closers*. The subject of the sentence is underlined <u>once</u>; the predicate, <u>twice</u>. Sentence-composing tools are **bolded**.

You may use five sentences for your position from the following "Sentence Bank," but you will need to find on your own at least ten more examples of that same position in nonfiction sources.

Note: To find your own sentences illustrating your position, you may search nonfiction titles from this worktext, or find other titles elsewhere. You may not, though, use any sentences from activities in this worktext, except for five from the fifteen in the Sentence Bank below.

SENTENCE BANK

OPENERS

1. **The youngest and only boy of four children,** Nelson and his father cared for the cattle and sheep.

   Barry Denenberg, *Nelson Mandela: No Easy Walk to Freedom*

2. **Worried that he would get stuck in the snow if he drove farther,** he stopped his rig on the crest of a low rise.

   Jon Krakauer, *Into the Wild*

3. **Using a new style of attack known as blitzkrieg, German for** *lightning war*, Hitler's planes, tanks, and soldiers slashed deep into Polish territory.

   Steve Sheinkin, *Bomb*

4. **As the helicopter came down between the pine trees and settled onto the bogs where the accident had occurred,** the smell of burned flesh hit Pete even before the hatch was completely open.

   Tom Wolfe, *The Right Stuff*

5. **While the American fliers were investing all their energies in land planes,** the Italians saw sea planes as the way of the future.

   Bill Bryson, *One Summer*

S-V SPLITS

6. Talloi, **breathing hard and speaking slowly**, asked why they were back.

   Ishmael Beah, *A Long Way Gone*

7. Arrowhead crabs, **bright spiderlike reef creatures familiar to scuba-divers**, have eyes set so far apart they can see in almost a complete circle.

   Diane Ackerman, *A Natural History of the Senses*

8. Nancy Gunter, **who was in charge of the astronaut crew quarters in the operations and checkout building**, came to work before midnight.

   Hugh Harris, *Challenger*

9. A thousand pages, **loosely bound and with no two sheets quite matching**, was an unwieldy load requiring both arms to carry.

   Bill Bryson, *Shakespeare*

10. Chung, **the daughter of South Korean immigrants and a passionate advocate for human rights**, launched a project in South Florida to represent mentally incompetent immigrants facing deportation.

    Sonia Nazario, *Enrique's Journey*

CLOSERS

11. All morning my mother had been scolding me, **telling me to keep still, warning me that I must make no noise**.

    Richard Wright, *Black Boy*

12. Sharks glided in lazy loops around their rafts, **dragging their backs along the rafts, waiting**.

    Laura Hillenbrand, *Unbroken*

13. The town's natives <u>did their shopping on King Street</u>, **the town's shopping strip, a slice of chain department stores, auto dealerships, fast-food restaurants**.

Tracy Kidder, Home Town

14. She <u>was an accomplished violinist</u>, **far out of the ordinary in fact, her talent so highly valued in her home that growing up she never had to do the dishes for fear that her fingers would be damaged by soap and water**.

Daniel James Brown, The Boys in the Boat

15. The pilot <u>was busy</u>, **trying to restart the engine, working to raise somebody on the radio, reviewing emergency procedures, keeping the right glide angle to hold the plane in the air as long as possible and yet maintain flying speed, trying all the while to locate a place suitable for an emergency landing**.

Gary Paulsen, Guts

- -

PART THREE: DUPLICATING EARLIER ACTIVITIES

To teach your position, use the same formats as the three activities described below: *matching, combining, imitating*. Also use the same directions, but use only new sentences from the Sentence Bank—plus more nonfiction sentences you find independently (not from this worktext).

- -

ACTIVITY 1: MATCHING

First study and then duplicate how a matching activity is set up for the position you're teaching. Use exactly the same directions.

opener (page 49)

S-V split (page 56)

closer (page 63)

ACTIVITY 2: COMBINING

First study and then duplicate how a combining activity is set up for the position you're teaching. Use exactly the same directions.

opener (page 49)

S-V split (page 57)

closer (page 63)

ACTIVITY 3: IMITATING

First study and then duplicate how an imitating activity is set up for the position you're teaching. Use exactly the same directions.

opener (page 51)

S-V split (page 58)

closer (page 65)

PART FOUR: TEACHING YOUR ACTIVITIES

Teach your three activities—*matching, combining, imitating*—to members of your own class—just a few or all members.

Use any effective method: whiteboard, video, website, overhead, PowerPoint—or some other effective presentation.

- -

While we teach, we learn.

—Seneca, philosopher

- -

T
E
LEARN
C
H